222 Recipes *the* GREEK Cookery Book

MICHALIS TOUMBIS PUBLICATIONS S.A. - ATHENS

Texts - Recipes by: SOFIA SOULI
Presentation of recipes: XENI KANELLOPOULOU
Translation: IDA ORNSTEIN
Edited: COX & SOLMAN

Colour design: YANNIS KOLLAROS
Artwork: NORA ANASTASOGLOU
Photosetting: KIKI SANTORINEOU
Montage: NIKOS PRASSIANAKIS
Printed by: M. TOUMBIS GRAPHIC ARTS S.A., Athens - Tel. 9923874

mail toubis@compulink.gr

The Minoan fisherman of Santorini (mural). Since time immemorial fishermen have used the same technique to fish the blue waters of the Aegean — still an inexhaustible source of fresh sea-food today.

Just to get you started

One of the reasons why Greece was inhabited very early in human history was that its geographical position and climatic conditions combined to provide security and guarantee a steady supply of food. It is this friendly environment which continues today to be the country's principal feature. There is sun to caress the vine and the olive and ripen the crops. There is rain to soften the earth, making it ready to accept the seed, and there is snow on the high mountains which, when it melts, sends down rivers to water the fields. And so for centuries the soil of Greece has been generous in giving man its products: juicy fruit in a thousand varieties and colours, vegetables, cereals, pulses, herbs and spices. There can, of course, be no comparison with the quantities of food produced in some other countries, but the richness of Greek earth and the singular morphology of the terrain give the country's fruit and vegetables a taste and quality rivalled nowhere in the world. And the sea, which is never far away wherever one is in Greece, is another inexhaustible source of delicious and nourishing food.

The nation which has inhabited Greece for all those millenia has adapted its neéds to the natural environment and over the centuries has developed a unique combination of tastes and forms of presentation. The rich and carefully-prepared meals served on feast days or at wedeings alternate with more spartan fare which is still nourishing, healthy and good to eat.

In a country where the intellect first flowered and where the principles of the arts and philosophy were first worked out, it comes as no surprise to find that great care was lavished on the table around which the 'symposium' would be held. The wine which loosened the tongues of the distinguished guests accompanied equally exquisite dishes. But more than anywhere else in the Greek world, it was in Ionia that the art of taste reached its sublimest heights. The Greeks put down their roots in Asia Minor in very ancient times and prospered, gaining economic strength and creating a brilliant culture. Each home had its own kitchen, with an oven for making bread; that kitchen would turn out food of tremendous variety, with combinations of materials and tastes depending on the season and the time of day at which the dish was to be served. For the Greeks of Ionia, food was a ceremony in which cooks, servants and maids all had their parts to play. Eating was an integral part of their culture and reflected their high standard of living.

In the centuries which followed, the Greek ships which criss-crossed the Aegean brought Ionia nearer to the islands. Most of the islanders of the Aegean had family and friends 'across the sea' and the merchants of Chios, Lesbos, Naxos and Mykonos, to name just a few of the islands, seized every opportunity to develop trade with Asia Minor. At the same time as their commercial horizons opened up, they also became involved in a process of 'give and take' in cuisine. That is the reason why, when the Greeks of Asia Minor came to Greece in the 20th century, many of their traditional recipes had been known for generations in the islands.

As time passed, their features became interwoven with the culinary customs of central and western Greece, areas which had their own lengthy traditions stretching back to Byzantine times. From there, the network of contact and influence spread to the Ionian Islands, where it encountered Western cuisine and the innovation of the Renaissance. That is why a gastronomic journey round Greece is so fascinating; at every turn, travelling north and south, east and west, one comes across new and exciting ideas and tastes.

Many people are under the impression that the marvellous world of taste to be found in Greek cooking today is of Turkish origin. However, just a little thought and historical research will suffice to show that when the nomadic Turks arrived to settle along the coasts of Asia Minor, all they can have brought with them is the roughly-cured meat on which they lived. An existence on horseback does not favour the growth of delicate cooking, and organised households centring around their kitchens, with utensils and a proper oven, presuppose a settled way of life. Of course, there can be no denying that when the Turks reached Asia Minor they were quick to learn what the land could provide. Thus they became familiar with all its gastronomic delights, enriching them —and sometimes distorting them— with elements from their own culture.

Today, the Greek table can boast of a vast range of main dishes, appetizers and sweets. Of course, the country now also has abundant restaurants where food from all over the world can be sampled. But when we talk of 'Greek cooking' what we mean is the way in which the products of the earth of that country can be combined at the particular time of year. Needless to say, the deep freeze and the other ways of preserving food have put an end to the entirely 'seasonal' nature of Greek food, but it is no coincidence that we continue to think about refreshing dishes in the summer and hot soups in the winter.

For this book we have brought together 168 of the most characteristic Greek recipes. The main body of the collection is supplemented with 12 traditional festive recipes, 25 local specialities, 17 of the most typical Greek sweets and some pages with useful background information. We have also included 150 colour photographs which, we hope, will help cooks make up their minds on the aesthetic question of presentation. The recipes we have chosen are the most representative, but of course there are countless variations on them. Cooking is an art, and this book provides an opportunity for every cook to use his or her creative imagination, adapting the recipes to personal taste.

As an additional aid we have indicated the number of calories each helping contains; there are few things worse than cookery books which do not help one stick to one's daily programme of nutrition. In some cases, we have suggested a drink or other accompaniment for specific dishes. This is not intended to limit your choice; quite the reverse. In any case, in Greece every special meal has its starting-point in our own inclinations, in that delight in fun and enjoyment which the Greeks call 'kefi'. Let us hope, then, that our 'kefi' in writing the book will create 'kefi' as you cook our recipes and eat our meals!

Sofia Souli

Contents

Appetizers   *Mezedes*

'Mezedes' are the appetizers which precede any meal over which particular care has been lavished. They will also appear, to be nibbled on, at moments of relaxation and conviviality; drink, in Greece, is always served with something to eat.

The Greek cuisine is so rich in appetizers that there is a constant risk of never getting past them and on to the main dish; that, perhaps, is why the traditional school of meal-planning called for mezedes which were tasty but few in number: just enough to stimulate the appetite, not satisfy it. Today, of course, things have changed, and few households can afford the time required to prepare a full meal and a set of appetizers.

But a group of friends in a taverna by the sea, with a bottle of ouzo in front of them, will see the mezes in all its glory — the star of the table. In this chapter we have chosen a series of the tastiest Greek mezedes — as for the group of friends, that choice is yours! The materials used are those available on the Greek market, which, of course, means today the market almost anywhere in the world. With care and 'kefi', it will always be possible to turn out a little taste of Greece. To accompany these dishes, we suggest ouzo, the Greek aperitif, or retsina, the resinated wine which is so much a part of Greek life.

Yeia sas — to your health!

prawn salad
(garidosaláta)

1 portion (250 grms) calories: 300.

portions: 8

1	kilo of prawns
1/2	a kilo of potatoes
1/2	a cup of capers
5	hard-boiled eggs
1	cup of mayonaisse
	a few sprigs of parsley
	vinegar, salt

Wash, then boil the prawns without water, but with a little vinegar and salt for 15 minutes. Peel the potatoes, cut them into small cubes and then boil them, making sure they don't turn mushy. Cut the eggs into large pieces into a salad bowl, add the capers, the cleaned and boiled prawns and 2 spoonfuls of mayonaisse. Mix well and arrange in the bowl.
Pour the rest of the mayonaisse over this and garnish with the sprigs of parsley.

octopus, boiled
(htapódi vrastó)

1 portion (115 grms) calories: 220.
Cooking time: 60 minutes.

portions: 8-10

1	octopus (1 ½ kilos)
3/4	of a cup of olive oil
3	cloves of garlic
4	soupspoons of vinegar
	pepper, rigani

Wash the octopus well and place in a pan with no water. Allow to cook at a moderate heat in its own juices. Once the juices have been fully absorbed, add a little water if it hasn't softened sufficiently. After it has softened (cooked), drain and cut into pieces. Mix the rest of the ingredients and add to the octopus.

Variation: Parsley can be used instead of rigani.

octopus in wine
(htapódi krasáto)

1 portion (115 grms) calories: 411.
Cooking time: 60 minutes.

portions: 12-14

2	kilos of octopus
1	cup of olive oil
2	cups of dry red wine
	pepper

Clean octopus and cut into very small pieces. Place pieces in a pan with the oil and boil until moisture has been absorbed in the oil. Continue to cook on a low heat. Add pepper and wine and cook till octopus is tender and sauce has thickened.

Variation: You can, if you wish, add to the ingredients 4-5 whole tomatoes and 2 bay leaves.

fried mussels
(mídia tiganitá)

1 portion (6 mussels) calories: 720.
Cooking time: 10 minutes.

portions: 10

1 ½	kilos of mussels
3/4	cup of milk
1	egg, beaten
1	soupspoonful of oil
1	cup of flour
	salt, pepper
	oil for frying

Wash the mussels very well and open them with a sharp knife. Remove the contents of the shell and wash them again. Drain well. Mix the egg, milk and a spoonful of oil, salt and pepper. Add the flour and beat well until smooth. Allow the batter to stand for 1 hour. In the meantime, put a generous amount of oil into a frying pan and heat well. Dip the mussels one by one into the batter and drop in the hot oil to fry.

herring salad
(rengosaláta)

1 portion (130 grms) calories: 310.

portions: 8-10

4	herrings
1/2	kilo of potatoes
	milk
1	onion
4	soupspoons of olive oil
2	soupspoons of vinegar
1	green pepper
	parsley, finely chopped

Soak herrings in the milk for approximately 7-8 hours. Drain them and remove skin and bones. Then cut into small pieces. Boil the potatoes, remove the peel and cut into cubes. Slice the onion and pepper, mix in the parsley and add all this to the herring and mix together with the vinegar and oil.

Variation: You can, if you wish, leave out the green pepper and add instead slices of cooking apple, half a cup of yoghurt and dry mustard to the salad mixture.

Serving suggestion:
Garnish with slices of lemon and lettuce leaves.

lamb's pluck with rigani
(entósthia ladorígani)

1 portion (130 grms) calories: 340.
Cooking time: 50 minutes.

portions: 8-10

1	large lamb's pluck, or two small ones
1	onion, finely chopped
3	garlic cloves, finely chopped
1	cup of cooking oil
2	lemons
1	teaspoonful of flour
	rigani
	salt and pepper

Wash the pluck well and cut into pieces. Put into a frying pan with the oil, onion and garlic, adding the rigani, salt and the pepper. When the pluck has browned lightly all over, pour in enough water for final cooking. Finally, squeeze lemons into a bowl along with a spoonful of flour and one small cupful of water. Mix well and add to the liver, etc. shaking the pan. Allow to boil for 2-3 minutes.

'marinata' liver
(sikótakia marináta)

1 portion (130 grms) calories: 330.
Cooking time: 30 minutes.

portions: 6-8

1	kilo of calves' liver
1	cup of cooking oil
2	soupspoons of flour
2	soupspoons of vinegar
4	bay leaves
	a little rosemary
	flour, for frying
	salt, pepper

Slice the liver thinly after removing the skin and salt and pepper it. Allow to stand for a while. Pour oil into frying pan, flour the

stuffed spleen
(splína yemistí)

1 portion (130 grms) calories: 250.
Cooking time: 60-70 minutes.

portions: 6

1	medium-sized calf's spleen
1/2	cup of liver, finely chopped
5	cloves of garlic, crushed
1	onion, finely chopped
1	cup of tomato juice
1	cup of olive oil
	parsley, finely chopped
	salt
	pepper

Wash the spleen, make a cut (not too deep) on one side. Insert a sharp knife into this opening and turn it within the spleen, making sure the opposite side is not penetrated.

Pour the oil in a frying pan and add the chopped onion and crushed garlic. Add the liver and cook lightly, then add the tomato juice, parsley and salt and pepper. Allow to cook for 15-20 minutes until a thick sauce forms. Stuff the spleen with this mixture and sew up the opening with needle and thread. Place in a roasting tin, salt and pepper it and pour the rest of the oil around. Roast for 40-50 minutes. Serve cold, cut into slices.

Variation: Mince can be used instead of liver, if preferred.

liver and fry at a moderate heat, making sure the liver does not burn.

To the oil in the frying pan, add 2 spoonfuls of flour, mix well, add the vinegar, diluting with a little water, then add the bay leaves, the rosemary and the salt and the pepper. Allow the sauce to boil for a while, then pour over the liver when serving.

splinántero
(splinántero)

1 portion (130 grms) calories: 340.
Cooking time: 1-1½ hour.

portions: *10-12*

1	large intestine (lamb or goat)
2	sets of lamb offal (without lungs)
3-4	spleens and sets of the sweetbreads
6-7	cloves of garlic
	salt, pepper

Cut the offal into pieces. Add salt and pepper and the garlic, finely chopped. Stuff the intestine, which has been thoroughly washed before and has had one end tied. Finally, tie the other end and pass a spit through it, in advance, making sure that it turns evenly over the heat without burning. Cook till well browned, then remove and cut into pieces.

liver with onions
(sikóti me kremidákia)

1 portion (180 grms) calories: 650.
Cooking time: 50 minutes.

portions: *5-6*

1	kilo of calves' liver
1	kilo of small onions
1	cup of cooking oil
1	cup of dry white wine
1	cup of tomato juice
2	cloves
	salt, pepper

Cut the liver into slices, wash well and drain. Peel the onions, heat the oil in a frying pan and add the onions; cook until softened. Immediately add the liver, the 2 cloves and the salt and pepper. Turn them a few times to cook evenly, then pour in the wine along with tomato juice. Allow to boil till you have a sauce.

gardoúmba
(gardoúmba)

1 portion (115 grms) calories: 100.
Cooking time: 60 minutes.

portions: *10-12*

2	kilos of lambs' intestines
1	cup of olive oil
2	soupspoonfuls of butter
3	lemons
	rigani and allspice
	salt, pepper

Wash intestines very well, turning them inside-out. Salt them and rinse with lemon juice. Rinse again with clear water. Next, scald them well, then put them in a bowl. Add the allspice, the rigani and salt and pepper and mix together well.

After having separated the intestines into 4 lengths, plait each, ensuring that it has not been plaited too tightly. Place the plait in a pan. Add the oil and butter together with 2 glasses of water. Cook on a moderate heat for approximately 1 hour or until a sauce has formed.

Variation: You can make gardoúmba with lamb sweetbreads by plaiting the intestines, not too tightly, around the sweetbreads.

brawn
(pihtí)

1 portion (115 grms) calories: 220.
Cooking time: 90 minutes the first time.
30 minutes the second time.

1	pig's head (3-4 kilos)
4-5	cloves of garlic, thickly sliced
10	bay leaves
1	coffee cup of vinegar
	a small handful of whole peppercorns
	salt

For garnish: 2 hard-boiled eggs and 2 boiled carrots, sliced.

Clean the head well, remove the bristles, then boil well (not the bristles). Allow to cool and keep aside the juices. Remove the bones from the head, cut meat into cubes and return it to pan with the juices to re-boil. Add the garlic, the bay leaves, the vinegar, the peppercorns and the salt. Arrange the sliced carrots and eggs into a pleasing pattern in a mould, add the meat and cover with the juice. After cooling, place in fridge.

sarmas
(sarmás)

1 portion (130 grms) calories: 680.
Cooking time: 30 minutes.

portions: 6-8

1	small set of lamb's
1	outer 'veil' of fat from lamb
	a few sweetbreads
	a small portion of intestine
1	cup of rice
	parsley, mint, both finely chopped
2	soupspoonfuls of butter
1/2	kilo of onions, finely chopped
1	egg, salt, pepper

Cut into very small pieces, after they have been lightly boiled, the liver, the sweetbreads and the intestine. Put 1 spoonful of butter to heat in a small frying pan. Put in the onions and allow them to fry till lightly browned. Add the rest of the ingredients, constantly stirring. Add a little water and allow to boil for about 10 minutes. Next, spread the lamb fat in a deep, buttered roasting pan, leaving some excess over the sides. Pour the mixture in. Add 1 spoonful of butter and cover the mixture with the excess lamb 'veil'. Finally, coat with a beaten egg and bake for 20 minutes approximately.

cod croquettes
(bakaliáros kroketákia)

1 portion (4 croquettes) calories: 680.
Cooking time: 15 minutes.

portions: 10

1/2	kilo of filleted cod
1/2	kilo of mashed potato
1/2	cup of milk
1	cup of grated cheese
1	soupspoonful of butter
3	eggs
	salt, breadcrumbs, pepper and oil

Break the fish into pieces with a fork, then put into a frying pan with the mashed potatoes, butter, milk and pepper. Mix ingredients over a low heat for a short while until mixture thickens. Then remove from heat. Add one egg and one egg yolk and the cheese. Place in the fridge for 2-3 hours (covered). Then remove, form into croquettes and flour each one.

In separate bowl, beat 1 egg and one white of egg with a teaspoonful of oil. Dip each croquette into this mixture, then roll each one in the breadcrumbs. Fry in very hot oil. Serve hot, with garlic sauce (p. 20), garnished with sprigs of parsley and slices of lemon.

Variation: Nutmeg and finely chopped parsley can be added to the mixture.

fish roe croquettes
(taramokeftédes)

1 portion (4 croquettes) calories: 320.
Cooking time: 10 minutes.

portions: 10

150	grms of fish roe
1 ¼	cups of water
1 ¼	cups of plain flour
1	small onion, chopped
	a small quantity of dill
	oil

Dilute the roe in water adding all the other ingredients and finally blending in the flour until the mixture becomes thick. Put oil in a frying pan and allow it to get very hot. Reduce the heat and drop in the mixture with the aid of a spoon. Fry till lightly browned.

rigani croquettes
(riganokeftédes)

1 portion (4 croquettes) calories: 420.
Cooking time: 10 minutes.

portions: 10

1	kilo of potatoes
200	grms of fish roe
2	eggs, beaten
1	medium-sized onion, chopped
1	level soupspoon of rigani
	pepper, flour and oil

Boil the potatoes and remove peel. Before allowing them to get cold, purée in a blender. Add the roe, eggs and onion and the rigani and combine all ingredients well. Allow the mixture to thicken in the fridge. Then form it into croquettes and flour them. Then fry them in plenty of hot oil till lightly browned.

spiced onion croquettes
(kremmidokeftédes pikántiki)

1 portion (4 croquettes) calories: 280.
Cooking time: 10 minutes.

portions: 10

1/2   kilo of onions
1/2   kilo of self-raising flour
1   small handful of mint, chopped very finely
1   teaspoonful each of salt and pepper
      frying oil

Peel the onions then grate half of the amount, chopping the other half coarsely. Mix them with the flour and mint, salt and pepper and add warm water until it turns into a thick paste. Put oil in a frying pan and heat till very hot. Add a spoonful of the paste at a time till all are lightly browned.

courgette croquettes
(kolokithokeftédes)

1 portion (4 croquettes) calories: 400.
Cooking time: 10 minutes.

portions: 12

1   kilo of courgettes
200   grms of grated feta cheese
1/2   cup of grated kefalotiri cheese
2   potatoes, well boiled and mashed
3   eggs, beaten
1   slice of dry bread, crumbled
      mint, finely chopped
      salt, pepper, plain flour, cooking oil

Clean and cut both ends off the courgettes and remove skins, then grate finely. Salt them and leave them stand for one hour on kitchen paper to drain. Then put into a basin, add the eggs to the courgettes, the cheeses, the breadcrumbs, the mashed potatoes, the mint, pepper and 1 soups-poonful of flour. Put mixture in the fridge for a while, then shape into croquettes. Flour them, then place them in a frying pan in very hot oil. Fry for about 10 minutes.

croquette potatoes
(patatokeftédes)

1 portion (4 croquettes) calories: 360.
Cooking time: 10 minutes.

portions: 8

1   kilo of potatoes
300   grms of kefalotiri cheese
4   eggs
      salt, pepper
      frying oil

Boil the potatoes and peel them. Put through blender. Mix the cheese, the potato and the eggs, adding a little salt and pepper. Put oil in a frying pan and heat well. Shape the mixture into balls and flour them. Fry them evenly till lightly browned.

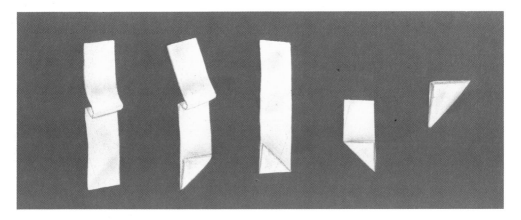

cheese pies (bite size)
(tiropitákia)

1 portion (5 cheese pies) calories: 320.
Cooking time: 15 minutes.

portions: 12

250	grms of feta cheese
1	cup of kefalograviera cheese, grated
500	grms of ready-made 'fyllo' pastry
1	cup of butter, melted
2	eggs lightly beaten
	parsley, finely chopped
	pepper

Mash the feta cheese with a fork, add the kefalograviera, the parsley, the eggs and the pepper.

Cut the pastry into strips of 6 centimetres wide, then cover with a cloth to keep moist.

One by one, brush each strip of pastry with the melted butter. Place a small spoonful of the filling on each strip of the pastry. Fold the pastry over the filling so that the end of the pastry forms a triangle. Keep folding into triangles as shown in the illustration. Butter a baking tin and bake them at a medium heat for approximately 15 minutes.

Variation: Wrap the cheese pies without having greased the pastry with butter, then deep fry them in oil. Remove them, draining off the oil by placing them on absorbent kitchen paper.

pastries with mince
(bourekákia me kimá)

1 portion (4 pastries) calories: 380.
Cooking time: 20 minutes.

portions: 12

1/2	kilo of mince
500	grms of ready-made 'fyllo' pastry
1/2	cup of white wine
1/2	cup of grated cheese
1	cup of butter
2	soupspoonfuls of breadcrumbs
1	spoonful of butter
1	medium-sized onion, finely chopped
1	egg, salt and pepper
	parsley, finely chopped

Place chopped onion and tablespoonful of butter in a frying pan and heat till onion has softened, stirring gently. Add the mince and when it has lightly browned, add the wine, salt and pepper, along with a little water. Cook gently for half an hour. In the meantime, beat the egg and mix in the parsley, the cheese and the breadcrumbs. Cut the pastry into strips approximately 15 centimetres wide. Brush with butter and put one spoonful of the mixture at the end of each strip. Fold each corner carefully over the mixture until you form a 'sausage' shape. Place them in a buttered baking pan, brush them with butter and bake in a medium oven for approximately 20 minutes.

baked haricot beans
(gígantes plakí)

1 portion (180 grms) calories: 410.
Cooking time: 45 minutes.

portions: 6

1/2	kilo of large dried haricot beans
3/4	cup of olive oil
1	medium-sized onion
3	cloves of garlic, chopped
3	ripe (or tinned) tomatoes
	parsley, finely chopped
	salt, pepper

Having soaked the beans overnight, change the water and boil till soft. Then drain and allow to dry for a while. Put the oil into a frying pan with chopped onion and garlic. If using fresh tomatoes, cut as fine as possible; add these to the pan along with the parsley. Bring the ingredients to the boil. Put the beans into an oven dish, pour over them the boiled sauce and bake in oven for three quarters of an hour, or until cooked.

Variation: If you wish, you can put all the ingredients into the roasting tin without having cooked them in the above manner; however, it takes longer this way.

fried courgettes
(kolokithákia tiganitá)

1 portion (150 grms) calories: 270.
Cooking time: 10 minutes.

portions: 8

1	kilo of large courgettes
1	cup of flour
1	cup of water
1	egg
1	tablespoonful of oil
	salt
	pepper

Wash the courgettes well and cut them into thin slices. Salt them and let them drain in a colander. Prepare a batter by beating together the flour and water, adding the rest of the ingredients. Put oil in a frying pan and heat very well. Dip each piece of courgette in the batter and then drop into frying oil. Fry both sides evenly until cooked. Serve hot.

Variation: Fried aubergines prepared in exactly the same way.

fried peppers
(piperiés tiganités)

1 portion (3 peppers) calories: 130.
Cooking time: 12 minutes.

1/2	kilo of long green peppers for frying
	oil for frying
	a little vinegar, salt

Wash the peppers well and allow to drain. Put the oil in a frying pan and heat well. Salt the peppers and put them in the hot oil. Once they have browned, turn them over to brown evenly on the other side. Remove them with care and salt them, then sprinkle with the vinegar.

Variation: The large fat variety of green peppers can be fried in the same way. They must, however, previously be punctured with a fork in a number of places.

garlic sauce
(skordaliá)

1 portion (130 grms) calories: 98.

portions: 4

1/2   cup of olive oil
5-6   cloves of garlic
      the middles of 5 slices of bread
      soaked in water
      vinegar
      salt

Peel the garlic and marinate in the vinegar for 5 hours. Crush the garlic and add the soaked bread, making sure that the water has been squeezed out. Put in 2-3 spoonfuls of vinegar and the salt and beat the mixture, adding the oil drop by drop. If the mixture appears too thick, add a little water and mix.

Serve garnished with olives and pickles on a shallow plate.

Variation: 1. Half a cup of walnuts, finely chopped, may be added, if desired.
2. Instead of bread, 5 medium-sized potatoes (boiled first, of course) can be used.

Garlic sauce is necessary accompaniment to fried cod and also goes wonderfully with fried courgettes and/or aubergines.

aubergine salad
(melitzanosaláta)

1 portion (130 grms) calories: 98.

portions: 6

1   kilo of aubergines
1   large lemon
1   cup of oil
1   small onion, finely chopped
1/2   cup of parsley, finely chopped
      salt

Puncture the aubergines with a fork and cook them in the oven till soft, with the skins slightly scorched. Follow this by mashing them along with the juice from the lemon and a little oil. To this beaten paste, add the onion, the parsley and the oil, drop by drop. To serve, garnish, if wished, with olives, finely sliced tomato and sprinkled parsley.

Variation: You can, if you wish, use 2-3 soupspoons of vinegar instead of the lemon and add to the ingredients 2 cloves of crushed garlic. For a variation on aubergine salad, add to the original recipe 1/2 cup of mayonnaise and 1/2 cup of yoghurt.

Tzatziki goes with souvlaki and all roast meats.

fish roe salad
(taramosaláta)

1 portion (130 grms) calories: 120.

portions: *3-4*

100 grms of fish roe
4 slices of bread
1 very small onion, finely chopped
1/2 cup of oil oil
2 juicy lemons

Soak the bread well and remove crusts. Mash well and add the fish roe. Taking care to work the mixture until it becomes smooth. Then, add the oil and lemon juice alternately drop by drop. If you want, add a little pepper. Place on small plates and garnish to your particular taste with olives or capers or pickles.

Variation: Instead of bread, you can, if you wish, use 4-5 medium-sized potatoes (boiled and mashed), or, if you prefer, instead of onion, 2 cloves of garlic, crushed.

Taramosalata is a favourite dish for fast days and goes down well as an appetizer with ouzo.

tzatziki
(tzatzíki)

1 portion (130 grms) calories: 75.

portions: *6*

1 ½ cups of yoghurt (strained)
2 medium-sized cucumbers
4-6 cloves of garlic, crushed
 a little vinegar
 salt

Skin the cucumbers and cut into thin strips with a vegetable grater; and then cut into small pieces. Drain and squeeze well and then salt. Add the crushed garlic, the vinegar, the yoghurt and mix, finally adding the oil. If you wish, you can sprinkle the tzatziki with paprika and garnish with olives.

Variation: You can, if you wish, add more garlic for a more garlicky taste, or, instead, add a mixture of finely chopped almonds and other nuts.

stuffed potatoes
(patátes yemistés)

1 portion (230 grms) calories: 350.
Cooking time: 60 minutes.

portions: 5

10	large, round potatoes
1/2	kilo of cheese, grated
1	onion, grated
1/2	cup of olive oil
1	tablespoonful of parsley, chopped fine
2	tablespoonfuls of butter
1	slice of rusk bread, crushed
	salt
	pepper

Clean and wash potatoes well. Remove potato filling, making sure that the skin has not been scraped so thin that it splits open later.

Put oil in a frying pan with the onion, the potato filling, the cheese, the parsley and the salt and pepper. Cook lightly and remove from heat. Stuff the skins with the mixture and place them in a roasting pan. Pour over the butter, coat with cheese and crushed rusk, add water to the pan till it reaches half way up the potatoes. Then roast them until done at a moderate heat.

Variation: Mince, if preferred, can be used instead of the potato filling, in which case replace the cheese with crushed tomato.

stuffed vine leaves
(dolmadákia yialanzí)

1 portion (5 dolmades) calories: 170.
Cooking time: 40-45 minutes.

portions: 10

50-60	vine leaves
1	cup of olive oil
1 1/2	cup of onions, finely chopped
1	cup of spring onions, finely chopped
1/2	cup of dill, finely chopped
1	cup of rice
	a good quantity of mint
	salt
	pepper
1-2	lemons

Scald the vine leaves, drain them and allow to cool. Mix all the ingredients except the lemon and wrap in the leaves forming them into 'roll' shapes. Place some of the vine leaves on the bottom of a pan, then place the dolmades in outward radiating circles, evenly spaced in the pan close to one another. Put a plate (not too heavy) on top of the dolmades. This is to ensure they don't break open during cooking. Add the juice of the lemon(s) and water, making sure the dolmades are covered. Boil slowly until the water has been absorbed and the rice cooked. Leave to cool.

fried cheese with egg
(saganáki me tirí ke avgá)

1 portion calories: 590.
Cooking time: 6-8 minutes.

portions: 1

1	*soupspoonful of butter*
100	*grms of kefalotiri pipperato, or other suitable frying cheese*
2	*eggs*
	a little flour
	salt
	pepper

In a small, round frying pan (a double-handled one is ideal), put the butter to melt and allow to heat very well. Cut the cheese into chunks and add to the frying pan. Once it has slightly browned, turn the cheese over to fry lightly on the other side. Then break the two eggs on to the fried cheese in pan. Sprinkle with salt and pepper and cook on a lowered heat till eggs are done.

Variation: Sausages (small or sliced) can be added to the cheese.

egg with tomato
(avgá me tomáta)

1 portion calories: 280.
Cooking time: 10 minutes.

portions: 3

6	*eggs*
5	*tomatoes*
1/2	*cup of cooking oil, salt, pepper*

Wash the tomatoes well, skin them and cut them up as finely as possible. Put the oil in a frying pan and once it has heated well, add the tomatoes. Salt and pepper them and allow to fry for 5 minutes until a sauce is obtained. In the meantime, beat the eggs well, then add to the tomatoes in the frying pan. Lower the heat and allow the omelette to cook well. Prick with a fork all over for better and even cooking. Then, when one side is done, turn the omelette carefully over to do the other side.

Variation: You can, if you wish, add potatoes to this recipe, but they have to be fried first before they are added to the egg and tomato.

Salads

*A good salad is certain
to make a fine dish
even finer.
This is where nature
comes into its own, with fresh,
cooling salads of raw vegetables
occupying the centre stage.
A careful presentation of freshly-
picked vegetables, with radishes to
stimulate the appetite and crunchy
peppers, is an irresistible temptation.
Apart from their colour and variety,
salads are of great value as
a source of the vitamins our
body needs so much.
We provide
a selection*

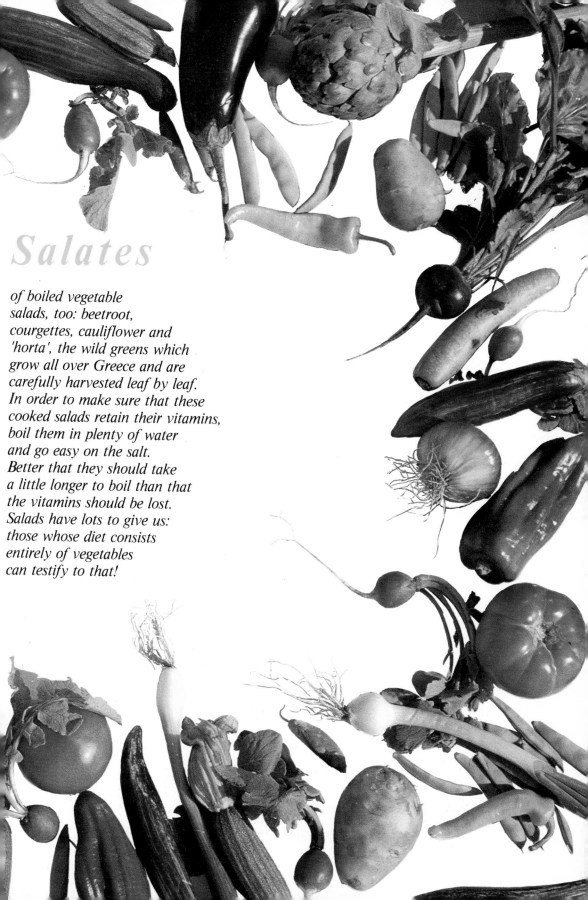

Salates

of boiled vegetable
salads, too: beetroot,
courgettes, cauliflower and
'horta', the wild greens which
grow all over Greece and are
carefully harvested leaf by leaf.
In order to make sure that these
cooked salads retain their vitamins,
boil them in plenty of water
and go easy on the salt.
Better that they should take
a little longer to boil than that
the vitamins should be lost.
Salads have lots to give us:
those whose diet consists
entirely of vegetables
can testify to that!

green bean salad
(ambelofásoula saláta)

1 portion (250 grms) calories: 320.
Cooking time: 20 minutes.

portions: 4

1	kilo of green beans
1/2	cup of oil and vinegar, mixed
	salt, pepper

Boil the beans for 20 minutes in salted water. Serve, when drained, with the oil and vinegar and, lastly, sprinkle with pepper.

Variation: 1. If wished, 3 cloves of garlic, crushed, can be added to the oil and vinegar mixture.
2. Can also be served with garlic sauce.

beetroot salad
(pantzária saláta)

1 portion (200 grms) calories: 200.
Cooking time: 50 minutes.

portions: 4

1	kilo of beetroots
	salt
	oil and vinegar

Clean and wash the beetroots. Remove the stems and the leaves. Boil the beetroots for 20 minutes, then add the leaves and boil for a further half hour. After this, strain them. Remove the outer skins from the beetroots while they are still hot, then cut into slices. Serve with oil and vinegar, or if preferred, with a garlic sauce.

potato salad
(patatosaláta)

1 portion, calories: 200.

portions: 5-6

1	kilo of potatoes
1/2	cup of olive oil
1	large lemon
1	large onion
1	small bunch of parsley
	salt, pepper

Wash the potatoes well and boil them in their skins for about 15 minutes. Then, before they have completely cooked, remove and peel them before allowing them to cool. Cut into round slices. Place them in a salad bowl, sprinkle salt and pepper over them. Squeeze the lemon and pour the juice over the potatoes. Cut the onion into fine slices, finely chop the parsley and add these to the potatoes. Add the oil, pouring it evenly all over. Mix the ingredients in the bowl.

Variation: You can, if you wish, use vinegar instead of lemon juice.

farmer's salad
(agrotikí saláta)

1 portion (150 grams), calories: 270

portions: 6

3	ripe tomatoes
1	cucumber
2	spring onions
2	hard-boiled eggs
	celery, finely chopped
1	clove of garlic, crushed
	parsley, lemon, salt, oil, vinegar
200	grms of feta cheese

Cut the tomatoes and cucumber into cubes and the onions into rings. Pour in 6 spoonfuls of oil and vinegar (mixed). Add to this the juice of one lemon, the celery, the parsley and the hard-boiled eggs. Finally, cut the cheese into slices and add to the salad.

lettuce salad
(maroulosaláta)

1 portion (180 grms), calories: 125.

portions: 3-4

1	large lettuce
4	spring onions
1	small bunch of dill
	salt, vinegar, oil

Remove the root and the outer leaves. Wash the rest with plenty of water. Cut as finely as desired. Cut the onions into rings and the dill finely. Salt the salad and serve with oil and vinegar (or lemon juice).

cauliflower salad
(kounoupídi saláta)

1 portion (300 grms), calories: 160.
Cooking time: 25 minutes.

portions: 5-6

1	cauliflower (2 kilos)
1/2	cup of olive oil
2-3	lemons
	salt

Clean the cauli and remove the stem, then re-wash well. Bring a pan of water to the boil, adding salt, then put the cauli in. Boil for 25 minutes approximately. Drain it and serve warm with oil and lemon juice.

boiled courgettes
(kolokithákia vrastá)

1 portion (200 grms), calories: 26.
Cooking time: 15 minutes.

portions: 5

1	kilo of medium-sized courgettes
	salt, vinegar, oil

Clean the courgettes and put into boiling salted water. Allow to cook for 15 minutes. Strain and serve cut in slices. Garnish with oil and vinegar.

cucumber yoghurt salad
(angoúri me giaoúrti saláta)

1 portion (130 grms), calories: 84

portions: 6

2	cucumbers
1	cup of yoghurt
1	onion, finely chopped
2	soupspoons of oil
1	spoonful of vinegar
	mint, finely chopped
	salt, pepper

bean salad
(fasólia saláta)

1 portion, calories: 405.

portions: 6-8

1/2	kilo of small dried haricot beans
2	large onions
1	bunch of parsley
2	cups of olive oil
1/2	cup of vinegar
	salt, pepper

Boil the beans well and strain. Cut the onions into fine slices and chop up the parsley finely. Put all the ingredients into a large salad bowl, add salt and pepper and mix well together, then pour the oil and the vinegar over.

mountain greens
(chórta tou vounoú)

1 portion (150 grms) with a little oil, calories: 140.
Cooking time: 30 minutes.

portions: 4-5

1	kilo of chicory greens or other wild greens
	salt, oil and lemon

Clean carefully and wash with plenty of water until all earth has been removed. Bring a pan of water to the boil and when it has put in the greens and cook till the water has turned green. There's no need to cover the pan while cooking. Boil for approximately 30 minutes, then strain and serve with oil and lemon juice.

Cut the cucumbers into small cubes and put into salad bowl. Add the onion, mint and the salt and pepper and mix well together.

Beat the yoghurt with the oil, the vinegar and a little salt and pour it over the other ingredients. Garnish with sprigs of fresh mint.

cabbage salad
(lachanosaláta)

1 portion (150 grms), calories: 50.

portions: 8-10

1   firm cabbage with small stem
     vinegar and oil
     or oil and lemon
     salt

With a very sharp knife or with a special vegetable grater, cut the cabbage very finely. Salt and allow to stand for a while.

Then serve in a deep salad bowl with either the oil and lemon juice poured over, or the vinegar and oil.

tri-coloured salad
(fréskia saláta tría chrómata)

You need a salad which has been prepared as above (cabbage salad)
1   *small red cabbage cut in the same way as described*
3   *large carrots grated and sprinkled with lemon juice*

Put all the ingredients into a salad bowl and sprinkle with lemon juice and oil (mixed) or oil and vinegar (mixed).

For garnish: cut radish into small pieces and place around the salad for an attractive presentation.

village salad
(choriátiki saláta)

1 portion (150 grms); calories: 260.

portions: 6

3	firm tomatoes
1	fresh cucumber
1	onion
2	green peppers
1	cup of black olives
180	grms of feta cheese
1/2	cup of olive oil
1/4	cup of vinegar
	rigani, salt and pepper

Cut the tomatoes and the cucumbers into slices and the onion and the peppers into rings. Place in salad bowl, sprinkle with salt, pepper and rigani and add the olives. Cut the feta cheese into chunks and add to other ingredients in the bowl. Pour over the oil and vinegar.

prawn salad

see appetizers...................... p. 10

herring salad

see appetizers...................... p. 11

aubergine salad

see appetizers...................... p. 20

fish roe salad

see appetizers...................... p.21

Pies

Any time of day is a good time for a slice of Greek pie, and, with its wealth of materials, this tasty dish can often be a meal in itself. The 'ready-made' pies sold by the shops on nearly every corner have, in recent years, perhaps led us to forget what real home-made pie tastes like. Yet making one's own 'pittes' is far from difficult.

This chapter gives simple recipes for home-made fyllo pastry. There is nothing particularly difficult about pastry, but for those who prefer not to take the trouble the shops can provide ready-made materials. All you have to do then is choose your recipe and put in the rest of the ingredients.

The best baking tins for the recipes which follow are medium-sized round or rectangular ones. In order to fill a large square baking tray like those which come with modern electric ovens, you will need double the quantities given here.
Happy baking!

dough for pie pastry I
(zími yia fíllo pítas I)

5	cups of plain white flour
5	soupspoons of oil
2 ½	cups of water
	a little salt
2	soupspoons of vinegar

Keep back part of the flour for flouring the board on which the pastry will be rolled out and with the rest of the flour combine the oil and add the salt along with the vinegar and water. Knead well and form dough into a ball. Allow to stand for approximately 1 hour in a cool place. On a floured surface roll out the dough into a flat sheet as thin as desired. This pastry dough can now be used for all your pies.

dough for pie pastry II
(zími yia fýlla pítas II)

1/2	kilo of flour
4	soupspoons of oil
1	teaspoonful of hard salt
1	cup of water

After having put aside a little of the flour for the rolling out of the dough, mix the rest with oil and the salt, combining loosely. Add the water to the dough kneading constantly on a floured surface. Allow to stand for 20-30 minutes in a warm place. After this, separate the dough into 6-8 balls, depending on the amounts and the thickness of the pastry you want to use.

shortcrust pastry
(zími sfoliáta)

500	grms of plain white flour
400	grms of fresh butter (unsalted)
1	cup of water
1	teaspoonful of salt
	juice of a lemon

Keep back a little of the flour. Put the rest into a small deep bowl. Make a 'well' in the centre of the flour and put in the salt, the juice of the lemon and the water. Knead it well and place it on a flat surface sprinkled with flour or water making sure it maintains its elasticity and also making sure it does not adhere to the hands. Then flour the dough, cover it and allow to stand in the fridge for half an hour. Shape the butter into an oblong and flour it. Roll out the dough into a thick, long sheet and put the butter on one half of it. Fold the other half of the sheet over it.

Put the floured dough on a floured surface and roll it out into a long sheet. Fold into

three. Roll it out again as before and do this four more times. Make sure that before it is rolled out each time it is well floured and is put in the fridge to stand for half an hour. Finally, roll out the dough into a bigger shape, flour it and fold into four.

It is now ready to be used for whatever kind of pie you wish.

cheese pie I
(tirópita I)

1 portion (1 large slice), calories: 360.
Cooking time: 45-55 minutes.

for a medium-sized baking tin

500	*grms of feta cheese, crumbled*
500	*grms of ready-made pastry,*
	or home made
1	*cup of kefalotiri cheese*
1	*cup of milk*
1	*cup of melted butter*
5	*eggs, beaten*
	parsley, finely chopped

Butter an oblong baking tin and spread over it the majority of the layers of 'fyllo' pastry, brushing each layer with butter. In a separate bowl mix the cheeses, the milk, the eggs and the parsley and finally the pepper. Empty the mixture into the baking tin and spread it evenly. Spread the rest of the pastry (buttered) over the top and then trim the edges. Bake the pie for 45-55 minutes at a moderate heat.

cheese pie II
(tirópita II)

1 portion (1 large slice), calories: 390.
Cooking time: 50-60 minutes.

for a medium-sized baking tin

300	*grms of feta cheese*
200	*grms of graviera cheese, grated*
1	*cup of butter*
3	*eggs, beaten, a little milk*
	bechamel sauce
	shortcrust pastry,
	or home-made 'fyllo'

Grease a medium-sized round baking tin with butter. Spread in it one part of the home-made crust pastry or three layers of 'fyllo' having buttered each one well. Prepare the bechamel sauce and mix this with the cheeses and the beaten eggs. Spread this mixture evenly in the tin and then spread the crust pastry over it, or two sheets of home-made 'fyllo' pastry. Brush the pie with a little milk, then bake in a moderate oven for about 50-60 minutes.

spinach pie
(spanakópita)

1 portion (1 large slice), calories: 300.
Cooking time: 50-60 minutes.

for a medium-sized baking tin

1	kilo of spinach
500	grms of pastry
300	grms of spring onions
1 ½	cups of olive oil
1	sprig of dill
	nutmeg, finely grated, salt, pepper

Wash the spinach well and remove the root and the hard stems. Cut up finely. Shake on salt and then rub vigorously with the fingers and squeeze to remove as much water as possible. What should remain is a softened mass of spinach. Clean the onions and slice finely; wash the dill and chop finely, then combine with the spinach adding the nutmeg and pepper. Mix well. Coat the tin with oil and spread most of the pastry, leaving enough to cover the tin after mixture has been put in. The pastry must be greased. Then spread the mixture evenly on the pastry which has been laid in the tin. Taking the left-over pastry (well greased), spread this over the tin and the mixture. Trim the edges of the pastry around the pan before baking the pie in a moderate oven for 50-60 minutes.

cheese and spinach pie
(spanakotirópita)

1 portion (1 large slice), calories: 400.
Cooking time: 60 minutes.

for a medium-sized baking tin

1	kilo of spinach
300	grms of feta cheese, crumbled
500	grms of pastry
300	grms of onions, finely chopped
1 ½	cups of oil
1 ½	cups of evaporated milk
1	sprig of dill, finely chopped
2	eggs, beaten
	salt, pepper, grated nutmeg

Wash the spinach well, removing the root and the hards stems, and cut finely. Salt the spinach well and squeeze, removing as much water as possible. Also squeeze to soften into a mass. Add the onions and the dill, the cheese, the milk and the eggs, the pepper, the nutmeg and half the oil.

Grease the baking tin with oil, then spread the pastry (well greased too) in the tin. Make sure there is enough pastry left over to cover the mixture. When the ingredients have been well combined, spread on the pastry in the tin evenly. Then spread the rest of the pastry over the mixture, greasing the outside of it. Bake in a moderate oven for approximately half an hour.

wild mountain greens pie
(chortópita)

1 portion (1 large slice), calories: 300.
Cooking time: 50-60 minutes.

for a medium-sized baking tin

1 ½ *kilos of assorted wild greens*
200 *grms of spring onions*
1 ½ *cups of oil*
1   *cup of feta cheese, 400 grms*
     (if wished)
     dill and parsley, both finely chopped
1   *soupspoonful of sugar*
     pastry

Clean and wash the greens very well and then cut up as finely as possible. Salt them and rub them vigorously between the fingers. Squeeze to remove as much water as possible. Add the sugar, the cup of oil, the dill and parsley and the cheese (if you are using it). Coat a baking tin with oil and spread the pastry in it, making sure this is well greased too. Take the greens and spread them evenly on the pastry, sprinkling them with oil. Take the rest of the pastry, grease this too and spread it over the mixture, then trim around the tin before baking the pie in a moderate oven for about 50-60 minutes.

courgette pie
(kolokithópita)

1 portion (1 large slice), calories: 360.
Cooking time: 45-55 minutes.

for a medium-sized baking tin

1   *kilo of courgettes*
500 *grms of home-made or ready-made*
     pastry
5   *medium-sized onions*
1/2 *cup of margarine*
1   *cup of olive oil*
2 ½ *cups of graviera cheese*
4   *eggs, beaten*
     parsley, salt and pepper

Clean the courgettes and cut them into small pieces. Boil them in salted water and strain well afterwards. Grate the onion and add to the pieces of courgette. Put all this into a frying pan and cook till all the juice from the courgettes has been absorbed. Add the margarine and allow to fry for a while. Then add the parsley, salt, pepper and, finally, the cheese and the eggs. Coat a baking tin with oil and spread most of the pastry, making sure enough is left over for spreading over the mixture. Grease the pastry too. Then spread the courgette mixture on the pastry evenly. Take the rest of the pastry and lay it over the mixture, grease this too, then trim the edges of the pastry before baking in a moderate oven for 45-55 minutes.

meat pie
(kreatópita)

1 portion (1 large slice), calories: 380.
Cooking time: 50-60 minutes.

for a medium-sized baking tin

500	grms of mince
500	grms of ready-made or home-made pastry
1 ½	cups of butter
1/2	cup of breadcrumbs
1/2	cup of dry white wine
4	onions
3	eggs, beaten
2	eggs, hard boiled, salt, pepper

Peel the onions and cut into thin slices. Put half the butter in a frying pan with the onions and fry until lightly browned. Add the mince and mix till the juice from the mince has been absorbed. Allow to stand for a short while then pour in the wine and cook slowly for 15-20 minutes. Remove from heat and allow to cool.

Cut the hard boiled eggs into pieces, add the breadcrumbs and the beaten eggs to the mince. Butter a baking tin and spread the greater part of the pastry in it, making sure enough is left over to cover the top; the pastry should be well greased. Put in the mince mixture, spreading it evenly over the pastry and then cover with the rest of the pastry which was left over. Trim the edges and butter the outside of the pastry before baking in a moderate oven for 50-60 minutes.

Variation for the filling of meat pie:

600	grms boiled lamb chopped into cubes
1 ½	cups of mezithra or anthotiro cheese (from Crete, if possible)
1	cup of buttermilk
3-4	spring onions, finely chopped ·
1	yolk of egg, mint, salt, pepper

Combine all the ingredients and use the filling for the same baking tin with the same proportions of pastry.

chicken pie
(kotópita)

1 portion (1 large slice), calories: 350.
Cooking time: 45-55 minutes.

for a medium-sized baking tin

1	chicken (1 kilo)
500	grms of home or ready-made pastry
1	cup of butter
1	cup of kefalograviera cheese
1	medium-sized onion
2	eggs, beaten
	parsley, finely chopped
	salt, pepper

Clean and wash the chicken and boil with the whole onion and salt. Boil it very well, taking care that about a cup of the chicken broth remains. Once the chicken has cooled, remove skin and bones, then cut into small pieces. Mix it with the cheese, the eggs, the parsley and the pepper and add to the ingredients the juice from the boiled chicken along with the softened onion, which has been lightly fried beforehand.

Butter baking tin and line it with most of the pastry, making sure enough is left over to cover the pie. The pastry should be well greased. Follow this by spreading the mixture on the pastry evenly. Then place nobs of butter at various points. Cover with the rest of the pastry, buttering the outside of it, and bake the chicken pie in a moderate oven for approximately 45-55 minutes.

cheese pies

see appetizers . . . . p. 17

onion pie

see local specialites. . . . . p. 135

Soups

Soupes

A plate of soup is not just a way of cramming into a single dish more beneficial ingredients than any single recipe normally contains: there are times when these liquids are the most delicious things we could possibly be offered.

Soup in Greece is thought of less as a beverage than as a complete meal. The range of soups runs from 'mayeiritsa', the special Easter soup, to Greek bean soup, a filling and tasty traditional dish.

Soup is often a pleasure in the summer too. Vegetable soup and tomato soup are both summer dishes in Greece, not only because they are light but also because the ingredients are cheap and easily available then.

The delicious and representative recipes which follow are worth working one's way through. The choice is up to you, and the right time is now!

fish soup
(psarósoupa)

1 portion, calories: 450.
Cooking time: 30-40 minutes.

portions: 6

1	fish (appropriate for boiling: gurnard, pike, sea bream or various types of rock fish)
8	medium-sized potatoes
4	small onions
3-4	small carrots
1	small bundle of celery
2	medium-sized ripe tomatoes
1	cup of oil
2-3	eggs
2	lemons
1	cup of rice
	salt

Choose a fish weighing about 1 kilo, remove the scales and gills and innards and wash the fish thoroughly, then salt it and allow it to stand. Peel the potatoes, scrape the carrots and skin the onions and put them whole into a saucepan, adding water to cover. Cut celery into pieces and add. Cut the tomatoes into quarters and put them into the saucepan too, adding the oil and salt. When the vegetables are almost done, supplement with more water and add the fish. Allow to stew for 20 minutes and then take the fish out, together with the vegetables. Place the fish on a flat dish, garnishing it with the vegetables, and strain the juice from the boiled fish to remove any bits, then boil again adding water if necessary. Then add the rice. Add salt if required or desired. When the rice is done, remove saucepan from heat and prepare the egg and lemon sauce.

Beat the eggs well and add the lemon juice drop by drop. Take to them a ladleful of fish stock and pour it slowly into the egg and lemon mixture constantly beating. Finally, add this mixture to the fish stock, stirring all the time.

greek bouillabaisse
(kakaviá)

1 portion, calories: 470.
Cooking time: 20-30 minutes.

portions: 8

1	kilo of various kinds of rock fish: sea perch, wrasse, streaked fish or scorpion fish
1	cup of various shellfish: mussels, cockles, oysters
2	carrots, 2 ripe tomatoes
1	stick of celery chopped
1	onion, 1/2 cup of oil
	lemon juice, salt, pepper

Clean the fish and wash them thoroughly. Cut up the onion, the tomatoes and the carrots into slices. Put the vegetables and the fish into a saucepan and brown in the oil. Then add water, ensuring that everything in the saucepan is covered by a good few inches of water, and allow to simmer for about 1 hour. Then strain the juice and mash the vegetables and the fish, after having removed the hard parts from fish. Put fish and vegetables back into the juice, together with the shellfish too. Allow to simmer together for about 20-30 minutes. Add salt and pepper. To be served with lemon juice.

lentil soup
(fakí soúpa)

1 portion, calories: 430.
Cooking time: 20-30 minutes.

portions: 4-6

1/2   kilo of lentils
1   medium-sized onion, finely chopped
8   cloves of garlic
1   cup of oil
4-5   tablespoonfuls of vinegar
1   cup of tomato juice
5   bay leaves
  salt, pepper

Pick over the lentils very carefully, making sure that all foreign bodies and bad lentils are removed and thrown away before washing. Wash them well. Put the lentils in a saucepan and cover with water. Allow to boil for 5 minutes, then strain. Put the lentils back into the saucepan with the onion, the oil, the tomato juice, the garlic and the bay leaves. Also add the vinegar and, finally, the salt and the pepper. Supplement with water according to preferred thickness of soup and allow the ingredients to boil till tender.

vegetable soup
(hortósoupa)

1 portion, calories: 178.
Cooking time: 20 minutes.

portions: 4-6

3   medium-sized potatoes
1   onion
3   medium size carrots
1   stick of celery, chopped
2   ripe tomatoes
2   small courgettes
1/2   cup of oil
  salt, pepper

Peel the potatoes and dice them. Do the same to the courgettes and the carrots. Cut the onion into slices. Skin the tomatoes and remove the seeds, cutting them into small sections. Put all the ingredients into a saucepan and cover with plenty of water. Add the oil, the salt and the pepper. Allow the soup to boil for 20 minutes. It can be served with lemon juice, if wished.

tomato soup with pasta
(tomatósoupa me zimarikó)

1 portion, calories: 240.
Cooking time: 30 minutes.

portions: 4

4   ripe tomatoes
1/2   cup of oil or 2 tablespoonfuls of butter
1 ½   cups of pasta suitable for soups
  salt

Wash and skin the tomatoes, removing the seeds, then chop them up. Put into a saucepan with the oil or butter (whichever you are using) and sufficient water. Add salt and allow to boil for 20 minutes. Then add the pasta and allow to simmer for 10 more minutes.

chick-pea soup
(revíthia soúpa)

1 portion, calories: 425.
Cooking time: 40-50 minutes.

portions: 4-6

1/2	kilo of chick-peas
1	large onion, finely chopped
1	cup of oil
1	tablespoonful of baking soda
	salt, pepper

Put the peas into water to soak overnight. Then strain them and put them in a bowl, mixing them well with the soda. Allow them to stand in the soda for about 1 hour, then wash them several times with plenty of running water to remove the soda. Put the peas in a saucepan with plenty of water and boil. When they come to boil, remove the scum which has formed on the surface and add the onion, the oil and the salt and pepper. Continue to boil till tender and soft.

bean soup
(fasoláda)

1 portion, calories: 470.
Cooking time: 60 minutes.

portions: 6

1/2	kilo of medium-sized haricot beans
4	medium size carrots
1	stick of celery
2	onions, finely sliced
1 ½	cups of tomato juice
1 ½	cups of oil; salt, pepper

Soak the beans in water overnight. Then allow them to boil for 5 minutes in the same water before pouring it away. Put the beans in a saucepan along with the carrots cut in thin rounds, the celery (finely chopped) and the onion and cover the ingredients with water. Add the tomato juice, the oil, the salt and the pepper. Allow to boil until all the ingredients are tender.

chicken soup
(kotósoupa)

1 portion, calories: 340.
Cooking time: 50-60 minutes.

portions: 5-6

1   chicken
1   cup of rice
2   eggs
2   lemons, salt

Put the chicken into a saucepan with plenty of water and allow to boil. Remove the scum which starts to form on the surface once it starts to boil. Then add salt. If the chicken is destined to be cooked in another way (frying, roasting, etc;), remove it from the stock 20 minutes later, but if you want it boiled, allow it to boil thoroughly. Once it has done and has been removed, add the rice. When the rice is ready, prepare the egg and lemon sauce. Beat the eggs well and add the lemon juice very gradually. Take a ladleful of stock from the boiled chicken and pour it slowly into the egg and lemon mixture, constantly stirring. Then add this to the stock again, stirring continually.

meat soup
(kreatósoupa)

1 portion (115 grms), calories: 220.
Cooking time: 60 minutes.

portions: 8-10

1   *piece of breast of veal, approximately from 1/2 to 1 kilo*
1   *cup of rice*
2   *lemons*
2   *eggs, salt*

Cover the meat with water and allow to boil. Remove the scum which forms on the surface with a perforated spoon and salt the meat. When the meat is well boiled, remove from the saucepan, strain the stock and add some more water to the required quantity. When it starts boiling again, put in the rice. (Where a thinner soup is preferred, add only half a cup of rice). When it is ready, remove soup from heat and prepare the egg and lemon sauce. Beat the eggs well and add the lemon juice drop by drop, beating constantly. Then pour the lemon-egg sauce into the saucepan with the stock again, stirring continually.

Variation: 1. Egg and lemon sauce can be omitted, if preferred.
2. 1½ cups of tomato juice can be used instead of the egg and lemon sauce. This can be added as soon as the scum has been removed when the meat comes to the boil.

easter soup

see festival dishes. . . . . p. 123

christmas soup

see festival dishes. . . . . p. 127

trachanas

see trachanas. . . . . p. 145

Sauces

When people talk of sauces, even when they know how important they are in giving the final touches to the taste, they tend to regard them as something extra, something non-essential. Of course, there are sauces which can be used or not, as desired, but there are many others which are absolutely necessary for the recipe.

This chapter gives a series of recipes for basic sauces. The quantities of ingredients are for amounts of sauce sufficient to meet the requirements of the recipes in which they are called for.

sauce for shrimps
(sáltsa yia garídes)

3   *tablespoonfuls of mustard*
3   *tablespoonfuls of oil*
     the juice of one large lemon
     salt, pepper

Mix these ingredients together and beat until they form a sauce. This is then poured over the shrimps.

oil and lemon sauce
(ladolémono)

1/2 *cup of oil*
2   *lemons*
     salt, pepper

Beat the juice of the lemons with the oil and the salt and pepper. To be served with boiled or grilled fish, salad and most shell-fish.

Variation: 1. Finely chopped parsley can be added if desired.
2. Lemon juice can be replaced by vinegar to accompany some vegetables or salads.

egg and lemon sauce
(avgolémono)

1   *cup of meat stock*
2   *eggs*
     juice of 2 lemons

Beat the eggs with the lemon juice, then add the stock to this slowly. Pour the sauce into a saucepan and stir slowly on a low heat, making sure it does not boil, because the egg will make it thicken.

Variation: 1. If the sauce is to be eaten as a soup, more stock can be added and as much lemon as desired.
2. If a thicker sauce is required, one more egg can be added to the basic recipe.

mayonaisse
(mayonésa)

2   *cups of good olive oil*
2   *egg yolks*
1   *teaspoonful of mustard powder*
     the juice of one large lemon
     salt
     white pepper

Beat together the egg yolks, the mustard powder, the salt, the pepper and a small quantity of the lemon juice. Blending the mixture constantly, add the oil drop by drop and when you have poured in the last of it, pour the rest of the lemon in too, also a little at time, constantly beating the mixture.

Variation: For a more rapid preparation of the mayonaisse, mix 2 level soupspoonfuls of cornflour, wait to allow it to cool and add the mustard powder, the egg yolks and the rest of the ingredients, adding more oil and lemon if wished. This mixture will thicken sooner if the oil is poured faster.

'marinati' sauce for fish
(sáltsa marináti yia psária)

preparation time: 5 minutes.
3   *tablespoonfuls of plain flour*
3   *cups of water*
1   *cup of vinegar*
3   *ripe tomatoes*
     rosemary
     salt, pepper

Using the oil that you have used for frying the fish, add the flour and brown it. Add the water, the vinegar, the tomatoes, which have been skinned and mashed beforehand, the rosemary, the salt and pepper and allow the mixture to come to the boil and thicken.

Variation: The tomatoes can be omitted if wished.

bechamel (white sauce)
for moussaka or macaroni pie
(sáltsa áspri - bechamél)

Preparation time: 15-20 minutes.

2   tablespoonfuls of good butter
2   heaped tablespoonfuls of flour
1/2   litre of milk
2   eggs
200   grms of grated cheese (kefalotiri)
        a little salt

Put the butter in a small saucepan to melt. Add the flour, stirring quickly with a wooden spoon to prevent lumps forming. Pour in the milk after having warmed it slightly first, and then add the cheese and salt, stirring the mixture constantly. When it thickens, remove from heat and allow to stand for one or two minutes. Beat the eggs and pour them slowly into the mixture, stirring continually. The sauce is ready for use.

Before it is baked with the moussaka or macaroni pie, sprinkle it with grated cheese to produce a crunchy surface.

pounded garlic sauce
(for appetizers and tripe)
(sáltsa skórdou)

Preparation time: 10 minutes.

4   cloves of garlic
1   cup of olive oil
3   heaped tablespoonfuls of flour
        vinegar
        salt

Put some of the flour in a saucepan to brown. Pound the garlic and the salt together and add the vinegar. Stir this in the saucepan, pouring in some water. As soon as it boils and thickens a little, the sauce is ready to be used.

tomato sauce I
(sáltsa tomátas I)

Preparation time: 60 minutes.

1   kilo of tomatoes
1/2   cup of olive oil
1   onion, grated
        salt, pepper

Heat the oil and when hot put in the grated onion. When it has softened, add the skinned and finely cut up tomatoes along with the salt and the pepper. Allow the sauce to simmer until all the moisture has been absorbed.

Variation: Finely chopped parsley may be added if wished.

tomato sauce with mince
(sáltsa tomátas me kimá)

Preparation time: 40 minutes.

1/2   kilo of mince
1/2   cup of olive oil
1   large onion, finely chopped
3-4   large, ripe tomatoes, or small skinned tinned ones
        salt
        pepper

Heat the oil and put in the chopped onion. When the onion has softened, add the mince and stir it until it is lightly browned. Then pour in the tomatoes (skinned, if fresh, and mashed), the salt and the pepper and allow to simmer till it thickens. To be served with pastas, or rice.

Variation: More taste and fragrance can be given to the mince sauce if desired by adding herbs or spices of your choice. (For example, parsley, basil, nutmeg, etc.).

tomato sauce II
(sáltsa tomátas II)

Preparation time: 60 minutes.

1/2   kilo of tomatoes
1   small onion
1/4   cup of olive oil
2   small sticks of cinnamon
        salt
        pepper

Put the onion, the skinned and finely chopped tomatoes with the other ingredients to boil, adding some water. Simmer on low heat for about 1 hour. Take out the onion and the cinnamon if you do not wish them to remain in the sauce when served.

tomato sauce III
(sáltsa tomátas III)

Preparation time: 50 minutes.

1   kilo of ripe tomatoes
3   cloves of garlic, finely chopped
1   small bunch of basil, finely chopped
2   teaspoonfuls of sugar
1/4   cup of oil or butter
        salt
        pepper

Wash the tomatoes, skin them and remove the stems and as many seeds as you possibly can, then mash them. Put into a small saucepan the butter (or oil) to heat, then add the chopped garlic. As soon as it softens, add the tomatoes, the basil, the salt and the pepper.

Allow to boil until it becomes a thick sauce.

sharp white sauce
(for: courgettes, fillings, stuffed vine and cabbage leaves)
(áspri xiní sáltsa)

Preparation time: 15 minutes.

3   tablespoonfuls of butter
3   tablespoonfuls of flour
3   cups of meat stock
2   eggs
        the juice of 2 lemons
        salt

Melt the butter in a saucepan and add the flour, stirring with a wooden spatula, and then pour in the stock and add the salt. When it thickens slightly, beat the eggs with lemon juice and pour them in little by little, stirring constantly on a low heat, without allowing to boil. In two minutes it will be ready.

Game and Poultry *Kynigi - Poulerik(*

Hunting was once a royal sport, and even today it retains its enthusiastic supporters. However, Greece has been considerably over-hunted in recent decades, and the pigeons, hares and boar which were once frequent visitors to the Greek table are now, in their wild form, extremely rare. Fortunately many of these birds and animals are now reared on game farms, the pro-

ducts of which are to be found in every supermarket. Even pheasant and quail are easy to buy. So even those who like putting on their crossed bandoliers and making for the mountains are likely to-

day to end up eating rabbit from the butcher's shop.

The recipes we have selected here are representative of the Greek approach to cooking game. We have also included a number of chicken recipes. As everyone knows, chicken meat is protein-rich and low in fats.

We hope these recipes give you more ideas for cooking game 'à la Grèque'. Both game and poultry are best accompanied by red wine — and if you attempt the hare 'stifado' recipe, make sure the wine is the strongest you can lay your hands on!

quails with rice
(ortíkia piláfi)

1 portion, calories: 620.
Cooking time: 60-70 minutes.

portions: 5-6

10-12 quails
1/2 cup of butter
1   onion, finely chopped
5   ripe tomatoes
2   cups of rice
     salt, pepper

Clean, singe and wash the quails very well. If they are very large, cut them in half. Salt and pepper them and fry in the butter. Put them in a saucepan with the butter from the frying pan and add the onion. When the onion has browned, add the skinned and crushed tomatoes. Allow the birds to boil for two or three minutes with the sauce and then supplement with 3 cups of water. Allow this to boil for a further 5-10 minutes and then add two more cups of water and then the rice. Lower the heat stirring now and then to avoid sticking.

When the water has been absorbed, and the rice is ready, serve it with freshly ground pepper.

young pigeons with wine
(pitsoúnia krasáta)

1 portion, calories: 300.
Cooking time: 50-60 minutes.

portions: 6

6	young pigeons
1	cup of red wine
1/2	cup of white wine
1/2	cup of butter
1/2	cup of oil
1 ½	cups of tomato juice
	salt, pepper

Clean the pigeons and singe them. Wash them and sprinkle with salt and pepper. Put them in a saucepan with the butter and brown them. Add the oil and immediately after, the red wine. Cover the saucepan for one minute. Then, add the tomatoes, skinned and crushed, and supplement the juice with 2 cups of water. Allow to simmer. Ten minutes before removing from the heat, add the white wine.

To be served with fried potatoes (chips) or spaghetti.

chicken with okra
(kotópoulo me bámies)

1 portion, calories: 470.
Cooking time: 60 minutes.

portions: 4

1	medium-sized chicken
1/2	kilo of okra
1	cup of oil
1	large onion
4	ripe tomatoes, skinned and crushed
	salt, pepper
	vinegar for the okra

Clean and wash the chicken well. Cut the onions into slices and put them in a pan with the oil to brown. Add the chicken. Make sure the chicken in the process of browning is turned regularly so that it browns evenly all over, then put in the crushed tomatoes.

Wash the okra well and remove the stem from the top end. Dip the okra pieces in the vinegar. When the chicken is almost ready, add the okra to it in the pan. Allow to boil until a thick gravy is formed.

Variation: The okra may be fried before being placed in the saucepan if desired.

rabbit casseroled in wine
(kounéli krasáto)

1 portion, calories: 480.
Cooking time: 50-60 minutes.

portions: 6

1	rabbit
2 ½	cups of red wine
3	onions, finely chopped
3	cloves of garlic, finely chopped
	parsley, finely chopped
1/2	teaspoonful of thyme
4	bay leaves
3	tablespoonfuls of flour
1	cup of butter; salt, pepper

Combine the wine with the onions, the garlic, the parsley, the thyme and the bay leaves. Chop the rabbit up into small portions and put it into the mixture. Allow it to stand in the mixture for at least 6 hours. After this, strain the portions of rabbit and fry them in the butter. As the meat is frying, sprinkle the pieces with the flour and, finally, pour over the mixture the wine and the herbs.

Add salt and pepper and 2 cups of water. Cover the pan tightly and allow it to simmer on a low heat until a spicy sauce has formed.

partidges with tomato sauce
(pérdikes me sáltsa tomáta)

1 portion (without the potatoes and rice),
calories: 270.
Cooking time: 50-60 minutes.

portions: 5-6

10-12 partidges
1/2 cup of butter
1/2 cup of dry, white wine
5 ripe tomatoes
salt, pepper

Clean the partidges, singe them and wash them well. Cut each one in half and salt and pepper them. Chop up the giblets finely. Put the butter in a flat, wide saucepan and brown the pieces of partidge on all sides evenly.

Add the giblets and stir. Immediately pour in the wine and half a cup of water. After having allowed to boil for about 1-2 minutes, add the tomatoes, skinned and crushed and without their seeds; put in salt and pepper and add 1 cup of hot water. Allow to simmer until all the water is absorbed and only the butter remains.

To be served with fried potatoes or rice.

hare casserole with onions
(lagós stifádo)

1 portion, calories: 850.
Cooking time: 60 minutes.

portions: 6-8

1 hare
1 1/2 kilos of small onions
1 large onion, finely chopped
4 ripe tomatoes
8 bay leaves
10 whole peppercorns
3 cups of oil, 2 cloves of garlic
1/2 wine glass of vinegar
salt, pepper, oil for frying

Remove carefully any stray hairs from the hare (no pun intended), without washing it. Cut it into small portions and allow to stand in its blood. Then put the hare with the finely chopped onions and the oil on to heat. Brown it, adding the whole peppercorns and the salt and the pepper. When the hare has browned sufficiently, pour in the vinegar and cover the pan immediately. Soon after, put in the tomatoes, which should have been skinned and crushed beforehand. Allow to boil for 1 or 2 minutes, then add the bay leaves and the garlic. Add enough water to cover and allow to simmer. Peel the small onions, which have been soaked in water and strain them. Fry them in a frying pan until they have browned and when the hare is almost ready, add these onions to it in the pan. Allow the boiling to continue on a moderate heat. The pan should be shaken from time to time to avoid sticking.

rabbit casserole with onions
(kounéli stifádo)

1 portion, calories: 800.
Cooking time: 60 minutes.

portions: 6-8

For the rabbit, use exactly the same ingredients as with the 'hare casserole with onions'. In this case, the rabbit must be washed very well before cooking.

lemon chicken
(kotópoulo lemonáto)

1 portion, calories: 480.
Cooking time: 60 minutes.

portions: 4

1	medium-sized chicken
1 1/2	kilos of potatoes
2	large lemons
1	cup of oil
	salt, pepper

Clean the chicken and wash it very well; salt and pepper it, then place it in a roasting tin. Peel and wash the potatoes, spread them around the chicken in the roasting tin and mix them with the lemon juice. Add the oil and 2 cups of water. Roast in the oven for approximately 1 hour, making sure it is turned so that it roasts all over evenly.

greek coq au vin
(kókoras krasátos)

1 portion, calories: 510.
Cooking time: 50-60 minutes.

portions: 4-5

1	capon, 1 1/2 kilos
1	cup of oil
1 1/2	kilos potatoes
2-3	tablespoons of butter
2	onions, finely chopped
1/2	cup of dry white wine
	salt, pepper
	cinnamon and 1 clove

Clean the bird well, wash it and then cut it into portions. Allow to drain and then coat the portions with flour. Put the butter in a frying pan and fry the portions.

Put into a saucepan the oil, the onions and the spices. Add the capon and, when they have browned together for a while, pour in the wine. Supplement the sauce with water and allow to boil.

chicken with rice
(kotópoulo me rízi)

1 portion, calories: 580.
Cooking time: 65 minutes.

portions: 4-5

1	medium-sized chicken
2	cups of rice
4	large, ripe tomatoes
1/2	cup of oil
1/2	cup of butter
	salt, pepper

Clean and wash the chicken well. Salt and pepper and coat the inside and outside with butter. Place the chicken in a roasting tin, adding the oil and 3 cups of water. Allow the chicken to roast for 45 minutes, turning it over now and then. Then add 1 cup of water (or more) and put in the rice. Add some salt and stir. Allow the bird to finish cooking in a moderate oven for 15-20 or more minutes.

Peel the potatoes, dice them and fry them. When the liquid in the saucepan is almost absorbed, add the potatoes. Remove from the heat after 3-4 minutes.

stuffed chicken
(kotópoulo yemistó)

1 portion, calories: 460.
Cooking time: 60 minutes.

portions: 5-6

1   chicken, 2 kilos
1   onion, finely chopped
1/2 cup of rice
1   cup of butter
2   cups of tomato juice
1/2 teaspoonful of powdered cinnamon
1/2 cup of almonds, blanched
1/4 cup of raisins
1   kilo of potatoes
     salt, pepper

Clean and wash the chicken well. Chop up the giblets and put half of the butter on to heat with the giblets and onion. Add salt and pepper and 1 cup of the tomato juice. Add the blanched almonds, the rice, the raisins and the cinnamon. Pour in a little water and allow to simmer for a while.

Peel the potatoes and salt and pepper them then spread them out in a roasting tin. Pour the other cup of tomato juice in.

Stuff the chicken with the mixture and sew the stuffed cavity up with a needle and thread. Coat the bird with butter and sprinkle with salt and pepper. Put the rest of the butter in the roasting tin. Add water and roast in a moderate oven.

chicken with noodles
(kotópoulo me hilopítes)

1 portion, calories: 520.
Cooking time: 60 minutes.

portions: 4-5

1   medium-sized chicken
1/2 kilo of noodles
4   ripe tomatoes
2   onions, finely chopped
1/2 cup of butter
     salt, pepper, cinnamon

Clean and wash the chicken and put it into a pan with the onions to brown. When it has browned all over, put in the tomatoes, skinned and crushed in a vegetable blender. Sprinkle with cinnamon and add salt and pepper. Bring to the boil on a moderate heat, adding 2 cups of water just before it reaches boiling point. Supplement the chicken stock with 2 more cups of water and when it starts to boil again, put in the noodles. Allow to continue boiling on a low heat until all the moisture (or at least most of it) is absorbed. To prevent the noodles from sticking, contents of the pan must be stirred frequently.

chicken pie

see pies . . . . p. 39

stuffed turkey

see festival dishes . . . . p. 127

Meta Meat

Meat   *Kreata*

Meat is man's basic source of proteins, those substances of which the human system has so much need to generate and regenerate tissue. That is perhaps why so many ways of cooking meat have been thought up. In Greece, lamb, beef and pork are the most commonly-eaten meats. Meat is stewed, roast or cooked in a thousand and one combinations with vegetables, which increase its nutritive content still further, or with spices and herbs to give it added taste. There are, however, certain traditional ways of dealing with each kind of meat. Lamb chops, for instance, are best when charcoal-grilled, pork can be superb when cooked with celery, and for 'stifado', the famous Greek meat and onion stew, beef will always be chosen.

This chapter contains some of the most characteristic Greek recipes, which also amount to a wide variety of different combinations of ingredients and cooking methods.

As for the drinks to accompany meat, we recommend a light red wine for veal dishes and a stronger red for charcoal-grilled, roast and cooked meat. And in the case of 'stifado', don't forget: bring out the oldest and strongest wine you've got in store!

stewed veal with potatoes
(moschári katsarólas me patátes)

1 portion, calories: 650.
Cooking time: 60-70 minutes.

portions: 4-5

1	*kilo of veal or tender beef*
1	*kilo of potatoes*
1/2	*cup of tomato juice*
1	*large onion, finely chopped*
1	*cup of oil*
	salt, pepper

Wash the meat and cut into small portions. Put into a saucepan with a little water and the onion to boil till all the water has been absorbed. Then, add the butter and allow to brown, making sure that the pieces of meat are turned so as to brown evenly. Add salt and pepper and the tomato juice. Add 2 more cups of water to the gravy which has formed and allow to stew. Peel the potatoes and dice them. When the veal is almost ready, add a cup of water and then the potatoes. Salt again.

When the potatoes have boiled and after the water has been absorbed and a gravy has formed, serve with freshly milled pepper.

braised veal with spaghetti
(moschári kokkinistó me makarónia)

1 portion, calories: 720.
Cooking time: 60-70 minutes.

portions: 4-5

1	*kilo of veal or tender beef, round steak or rump*
1	*large onion, finely chopped*
1/2	*cup of oil*
1/2	*cup of fresh butter*
1 1/2	*cups of small, crushed tomatoes*
1/2	*kilo of spaghetti*
6	*cloves of garlic, salt, pepper grated kefalotiri or parmesan — type cheese*

Make 6 holes in different parts of the meat and put into each hole salt, pepper and slivers of garlic. Do not cut up the meat. Put it on to heat with the oil and the onions and turn it so that it browns evenly on all sides. As soon as it has browned, put in the tomato juice and add supplementary water to this. Allow to stew. When the meat is ready (tender), fill a saucepan with water, putting in plenty of salt and put in the spaghetti to boil. When tender, drain the spaghetti and place it on a serving dish sprinkling it with the grated cheese. Put the fresh butter on to heat well, then pour it over the spaghetti.

Cut the meat into slices and serve with the spaghetti and its gravy.

braised beef with mashed potatoes
(moschári kokkinistó me pouré)

1 portion, calories: 680.
Cooking time: 60-70 minutes.

portions: 4-5

1	*kilo of lean beef*
1	*onion, finely chopped*
1	*cup of oil*
1 ½	*cups of tomato juice*
	salt, pepper

for the mashed potatoes:

1 ½	*kilos of potatoes*
3	*glasses of milk*
1/2	*cup of butter*

Cut the meat into portions, wash it well and drain. Heat the oil and put the onion with the meat into it. Brown the meat, add the salt, the pepper and the tomato juice. Allow the meat to stew, putting additional water in now and again.

Prepare the mashed pototatoes. Wash the potatoes well and allow them to boil without peeling. When boiled and cooled somewhat, peel them and then mash them with a potato masher. Heat the butter in a saucepan and add the mashed potatoes, stir a little, then add the milk and a little salt. Allow to cook for about 1 minute, remove from heat and serve with the meat.

tas kebab
(tas kebáb)

1 portion, calories: 490
(with rice), calories: 700.
Cooking time: 50 minutes.

portions: 6

1	*kilo of meat, either lamb or veal*
1/2	*kilo of onions*
1/2	*kilo of ripe tomatoes*
1/2	*cup of butter*
1/2	*cup of dry wine*
	parsley, finely chopped
	salt
	pepper

Dice the meat into medium-sized cubes, wash and drain. Put butter in a frying pan, heat it well and fry the meat cubes. Then put the meat into a saucepan. Cut the onions into slices and fry them in the butter. Then put the fried onions with the butter into the saucepan along with the meat. Heat, and before the ingredients begin to brown, pour in the wine and the tomatoes, which should have been skinned and mashed beforehand in a vegetable blender. Add salt, pepper and the parsley. Allow to stew, adding water if necessary.

To be served with rice, or mashed potatoes or even fried potatoes.

meat with vegetables
(kréas me hortariká)

1 portion, calories: 480.
Cooking time: 60-70 minutes.

portions: 4-5

1	kilo of veal or tender beef
1	head of celery
1/2	kilo of leeks
1	large onion, finely chopped
5	spring onions
1	small bunch of dill
1/2	cup of butter
3	ripe tomatoes

Wash the meat and cut it into small pieces. Put it on to the heat with the butter and the chopped onion to brown. Add salt and pepper. Wash the vegetables and slice them up small. Skin the tomatoes and crush them. When the meat is almost ready, add the vegetables and the tomatoes to the pan along with the meat. Add 2 cups of water and leave to finish stewing.

veal with courgettes
(moschári me kolokithákia)

1 portion, calories: 500.
Cooking time: 60-70 minutes.

portions: 4-5

1	kilo of veal or tender beef
1	kilo of small courgettes
1	large onion, finely chopped
1	tin of skinned tomatoes, crushed
1	cup of oil
	salt, pepper
	oil for frying

Wash the meat well and cut it into serving portions. Put the pieces of meat into a pan with the onion and half a cup of water. Make sure the meat is turned regularly and when the water has been absorbed, add the oil and allow the meat to brown. Add salt and pep-

veal tongue in wine
(moscharísia glóssa krasáti)

1 portion, calories: 400.
Cooking time: 60-70 minutes.

portions: 6-8

1	veal tongue, approximately 1 1/2 kilos
1	cup of oil
1	cup of dry, white wine
1	stick of celery
2	cloves of garlic
	salt, pepper

Clean and wash the tongue very well. Remove the hard parts which are at the root. Put water in a pan with the tongue and allow to boil for about twenty minutes. Keep the stock and drain the tongue. Remove the skin. Cut the tongue into slices and place pieces in a flat, wide frying pan with butter, which should have been heated beforehand. Salt and pepper the slices of meat. When the tongue has browned slightly on all sides, add the wine and cover at once.

A little while later, add the stock which you have kept, add the celery and the garlic in whole, peeled, cloves. Lower the heat and allow to stew until all water has been absorbed and a gravy has formed.

Remove the garlic and the celery and serve, either with fried potatoes and salad, or as an appetizer.

per and the skinned and crushed tomatoes. Add 2 more cups of water and allow to stew.

Clean and lightly scape the courgettes and salt them. Put oil into a frying pan and fry them so that they brown and a crisp surface forms. When the meat is almost ready, add the courgettes and leave to stew altogether.

stewed veal with peas
(moschári katsarólas me araká)

1 portion, calories: 590.
Cooking time: 50-60 minutes.

portions: 4-5

1   *kilo of lean veal or tender beef*
1   *cup of butter*
1/2 *cup of dry white wine*
     salt
     pepper
1   *teaspoonful of rubbed thyme*
1/2 *kilo of peas*

Wash the meat and cut it into slices. Heat the butter well in a wide, shallow pan. Salt and pepper the sliced pieces of meat and put them into the pan to brown. Pour in the wine as soon as it has browned and cover at once. Add the thyme and 2 cups of water and allow the meat to stew.

Boil the peas in salted water. When they are almost ready, drain and add them to the meat.

Allow to stew together for a while, then serve.

veal casserole with onions
(moschári stifádo)

1 portion, calories: 640.
Cooking time: 70 minutes.

portions: *4-5*

1	*kilo of veal (or beef)*
1 ½	*kilos of small onions*
6	*cloves of garlic*
1	*cup of oil*
1	*onion, finely chopped*
2-3	*tablespoonfuls of vinegar*
1 ½	*cups of tomato juice*
	salt, pepper
	bay leaves
8-10	*peppercorns*
	oil for frying

Cut the meat into small portions and put it into a pan with the finely chopped onion and the oil to heat. Turn the meat over a few times, browning it evenly. Add salt, pepper and the vinegar. Cover the pan for half a minute and then add the tomato juice, the garlic and the bay leaves and the peppercorns. Supplement the sauce with some water and allow the meat to stew.

In the meantime, peel the onions, after having soaked them in water, then drain and salt them. Fry them and then add them to the meat when it is ready. Allow to stew altogether until all moisture has been absorbed and only the sauce remains.

boiled beef
with vegetables
(vodinó vrastó me lachaniká)

1 portion, calories: 420.
Cooking time: 70-80 minutes.

portions: 6

1	kilo of beef (breast)
1/2	kilo of potatoes
1/4	kilo of carrots
3	large onions
4-5	courgettes
1	stick of celery
4	ripe tomatoes
	salt and red pepper

Put the meat, cut into serving portions into a saucepan and add water enough to reach the middle of the pan. When it starts to boil, remove the scum that has formed on the surface. Add salt and allow to boil on a high heat for at least 1 hour.

Peel the potatoes, clean the carrots, the onions and the courgettes and add these whole to the boiling beef. Add the celery as it is. Then add the tomatoes cut into four, salt and pepper.

When it is ready and the meat tender, serve in a deep serving dish along with the veggies, meat and gravy.

veal roll with cheese
(moschári tilictó me tirí)

1 portion, calories: 500.
Cooking time: 120 minutes.

portions: 6-8

1	kilo of veal shoulder
300	grms of feta cheese
	parsley, finely chopped
1	cup of butter
	salt
	pepper
	thyme
1/2	cup of red wine

Make sure that the piece of meat is almost square, so that it can be rolled up. Spread it flat, salt and pepper it and spread cheese in the centre lengthwise. Sprinkle the parsley on, roll up the meat tightly and tie it with string all round.

Put the butter in a flat, wide pan and heat. Brown the meat on all sides, add the wine and cover at once. Supplement the stock of the meat by adding 2 cups of water and put in the rubbed thyme. Allow to stew for 2 hours.

pork with cabbage
(hirinó me láchano)

1 portion, calories: 540.
Cooking time: 60-70 minutes.

portions: 5

1	kilo of pork
1	cabbage of 1 ½ kilos
2	large onions
1	cup of oil
1 ½	cups of tomato juice
	salt, pepper

Wash the meat and cut into small pieces. Heat the oil in a pan and cut the onions into slices. Put them into the oil and add the meat to brown. Then pour in the tomato juice, adding the salt and pepper too. Add 2 cups of water and allow to boil.

Cut the cabbage into large chunks and wash well. When the meat is almost ready, add 2 more cups of water, salt, pepper and the cabbage. Allow to boil together until the cabbage has softened completely.

To be served with freshly milled pepper.

pork with leeks
(hirinó me prássa)

1 portion, calories: 660.
Cooking time: 60 minutes.

portions: 5

1	kilo of pork
1 ½	kilos of leeks
2	small onions, finely chopped
1	cup of oil
1 ½	cups of tomato juice
	salt
	pepper

Clean the leeks and wash well. Cut them into 4-5 sections each. Scald them in salty water. Take them out immediately and allow them to drain.

pork with celery
(hirinó me sélino)

1 portion, calories: 700.
Cooking time: 60 minutes.

portions: 5

1	kilo of pork
1	kilo of celery
2	large onions, finely chopped
1/2	cup of butter
2	lemons
2	eggs
	salt, pepper

Clean the celery and wash it well. Chop it up into large pieces and allow to boil in salty water. Drain it before it is completely boiled and let it stand. Cut the meat into serving portions and put it into a pan along with the onions and a little water, heat and turn them over now and then. When the water has been aborbed, add the butter. Lightly brown. Add 3 cups of water, salt and pepper and allow to simmer on a moderate heat. When the meat is half cooked, put the celery into the pan to cook together. When this is well done, prepare the egg and lemon sauce. Beat the eggs, pouring in the juice of the lemon, beating all the time, then immediately add 2 cups of the meat stock. When it is well combined, pour this mixture into the saucepan. Shake the pan to distribute the sauce.

Cut the meat into pieces, salting and peppering it and putting it into a pan with the oil and the onion to brown. When the meat has lightly browned on all sides, add the tomato juice and 2 cups of water and allow to stew. When it is almost ready, add the leeks to stew together until a gravy has formed.

pork chops in wine
(hirinés brizóles krasátes)

1 portion, calories: 600.
Cooking time: 30 minutes.

portions: 5

5   *pork chops, without too much fat*
1   *cup of good oil*
1   *cup of dry white wine*
    salt, pepper

Salt and pepper the chops and fry them in a frying pan. When they are browned on all sides, add 1 cup of water and allow them to cook slowly.

When there is only oil left after the water has been absorbed, pour in the wine and cover. Allow it to stand for 1 minute before serving.

pork with beans
(hirinó me fasólia)

1 portion, calories: 790.
Cooking time: 60-70 minutes.

portions: 6-7

1 ½   *kilos of pork*
1/2   *kilo of dried beans*
1   *large onion, finely chopped*
1   *cup of oil*
      salt, pepper

Cut the meat into portions and heat it with the onions to brown. Add salt and pepper and the tomato juice. Allow the meat to stew. Boil the beans and drain them.

When the meat is almost tender, supplement the sauce with some water and add the beans. Allow to simmer together until the water is absorbed and you have a thick sauce.

Variation: 1. You can, if preferred, use large dried haricot beans.
2. This dish can be cooked in the oven, that is if you wish to avoid the bother of browning the ingredients.

roast leg of pork
(hirinó boúti psitó)

1 portion, calories: 480.
Cooking time: 120 minutes.

portions: 8-10

1   *small pork leg with skin*
2   *lemons*
6   *cloves of garlic*
1   *cup of butter*
    salt, pepper
2   *kilos of small, round potatoes*

Wash the pork leg thoroughly and remove any bristles. Make 6 deep holes with a sharp knife, fill them with salt and pepper and plug 1 clove of garlic in each one. Coat the pork leg with butter to obtain crunchy crackling.

Prepare the potatoes, peel them and sprinkle them with salt and pepper, add the lemon juice and spread them around the meat in a roasting tin.

Allow to roast slowly in the oven for at least 2 hours, turning the meat regularly.

souvlaki with pitta bread
(souvláki me píta)

1 portion (1 souvlaki), calories: 300.
Cooking time: 20-30 minutes.

portions: 8

300   *grms of lean meat (pork shoulder)*
8   *pitta breads*
8   *small skewers*
2   *onions*
2   *firm tomatoes*
    parsley
    rigani
    salt
    pepper (black and red)
1/4   *cup of butter*

Variation: Tzatziki (see p. 21) can be added to the contents of the pitta.

Wash the meat well, dice it and sprinkle with salt, pepper and rigani. Divide the pieces of meat into eight and put them on to the skewers individually. Put them to cook on the grill.

Chop the onions and the parsley. Wash the tomatoes and cut up them into thin slices. Cook the pittas one by one on the grill, coating them with butter.

When the pieces of meat are tender, put them on to the pitta (one skewer for each pitta bread) and slowly draw out the skewer leaving the pieces of meat in the pitta. Add the onion, the parsley, the tomato, sprinkle with red pepper and roll up the pitta having first laid it on greaseproof paper, so that when you roll them up, you roll the paper with them. Only half of the pittas is to be exposed above the grease proofpaper.

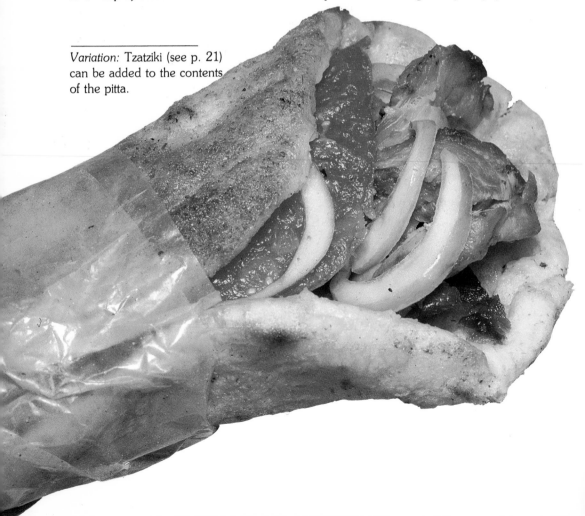

fried lamb with vinegar
(arní xidáto sto tigáni)

1 portion, calories: 670.
Cooking time: 50-60 minutes.

portions: 5

1	kilo of leg of lamb
1	cup of vinegar
3	tablespoonfuls of flour
1/2	cup of oil
1	heaped tablespoonful of butter
4	cloves of garlic, finely chopped
	salt, pepper

Cut the meat into thin slices, coat them with flour and fry them in the oil and butter. Then put it into a saucepan. To the oil and the butter from the frying add the garlic, the vinegar and 1 tablespoonful of flour, which you blend in thoroughly. Add salt and pepper; after the sauce has boiled, pour it over the meat. Allow the meat to cook on a moderate heat in the sauce, taking care that it doesn't stick.

To be served with vegetables or village salad.

lamb with lemon
(arnáki lemonáto katsarólas)

1 portion, calories: 790.
Cooking time: 60 minutes.

portions: 5-6

1	kilo of leg of lamb
1/2	cup of butter
2	lemons
1	kilo of small, round potatoes
	salt, pepper

Cut the lamb into serving portions and wash it carefully. Drain it well. Put the lamb and the butter in a pan and add salt and pepper. Turn it to brown evenly and then add the lemon juice. As soon as the lemon juice has been added, cover for 1 minute.

Add 2 cups of water and cover again, lowering the heat. Allow to stew slowly. Peel and wash the potatoes. Fry them in plenty of oil and when the lamb is tender, add the potatoes to the pan. Add more salt and a little more water and allow to simmer for 10 more minutes. To be served with freshly milled pepper.

lamb with rice
(arnáki atzém piláfi)

1 portion, calories: 780.
Cooking time: 50-60 minutes.

portions: 4-6

1	kilo of lamb, top side
1	tin of skinned tomatoes
1	cup of butter
1	onion, finely chopped
2	cups of rice
	salt, pepper

Wash the lamb and cut into very small portions. Put the portions into a saucepan with the finely chopped onion and heat until all moisture has been absorbed. Then immediately add the butter.

When it browns, put in salt and pepper and add the mashed tomatoes, supplementing the sauce by adding 2 cups of water. Just before the lamb becomes tender, add the rice. Lower the heat and allow to simmer. When all the water has been absorbed, serve with freshly milled pepper.

lamb fricassé with lettuce
(arnáki fricassé me maroúlia)

1 portion, calories: 670.
Cooking time: 60 minutes.

portions: 5

1	kilo of lamb (shoulder or breast)
300	grms of spring onions finely chopped
3	lettuces
1	small bunch of dill, finely chopped
1/2	cup of butter
2	lemons
2	eggs
	salt, pepper

Cut the meat into medium-sized portions and wash them well. Heat them in a pan with the onions, stirring occasionally. When the moisture has been absorbed, add a little butter, the dill and the salt and pepper. Leave the pieces of meat in the butter for a while, long enough to soften and brown the onions. The meat must not brown. Then immediately add 2 cups of water and allow to boil slowly.

In the meantime, wash the lettuces and coarsely shred them. Boil them in salty water then strain. When the lamb is ready, put them in the saucepan and allow to boil for 2-3 minutes with the meat.

roast lamb with potatoes
(arní me patátes sto foúrno)

1 portion, calories: 720.
Cooking time: 60-70 minutes.

portions: 6-7

1 ½	kilos of leg of lamb
1 ½	kilo of potatoes
1	cup of butter or oil
2	lemons
	salt, pepper

Peel the potatoes and dice them or cut them into long narrow slices. Wash them and sprinkle them with salt and pepper and the lemon juice, mixing them together and then spreading them in the roasting tin. Add the butter or the oil and 2 cups of water. Put the lamb in with the potatoes and roast in a fairly hot oven to begin with, but reducing the heat after a short while.

When the meat is browned on one side, turn it and roast the other side. About one hour and ten minutes is required for the meat to become tender.

Variation: If desired, pierce holes in the leg of lamb in 4-5 places and plug the holes with cloves of garlic which have been salted and peppered well.

Remove from heat and prepare the egg and lemon sauce. Beat the eggs well and add the lemon juice drop by drop. Take 1-2 cups of the meat stock and add it slowly to the sauce. Then add this sauce to the meat in the pan. Shake the saucepan to distribute the sauce over the meat.

lamb with aubergines
(arnáki me melitzánes)

1 portion, calories: 790.
Frying time: 10 minutes
Cooking time: 60 minutes.

portions: 5-6

1	kilo of lamb
1	kilo of long, narrow aubergines
1	large onion, finely chopped
1/2	cup of oil
	salt, pepper
	oil for frying

Cut the lamb into portions and wash it well. Put it into a pan with the onion and the oil. Salt and pepper it, turning it occasionally to brown evenly on all sides. Then put in the skinned and crushed tomatoes, add water and allow it to simmer. Peel the aubergines, wash them and cut them into large, round pieces. Salt them and allow them to drain for a short while.

Heat the oil and fry them slightly. When the lamb is almost ready, add the aubergines and some water (if necessary) and allow to complete cooking.

To be served with freshly milled pepper.

lamb with artichokes and egg and lemon sauce
(arnáki me aggináres avgolémono)

1 portion, calories: 720.
Cooking time: 60 minutes.

portions: 4

1	kilo of lamb
8	artichokes
1/2	cup of butter
5	spring onions, finely chopped
1	small bunch of dill
2	eggs
2	lemons
	salt, pepper

Cut the lamb into serving portions, wash them and drain. Put it into a pan with the finely chopped onion and cook and stir till all its moisture has been absorbed. Put the butter, the dill, the salt and the pepper into the saucepan and brown the lamb lightly. When it has browned evenly on all sides, add 2-3 cups of water and allow to cook slowly.

Take the artichokes and remove the tough, outer leaves, remove most of the stems and pull out the leaves surrounding the hearts. Scrape out the hairy centres. Rub the hearts with lemon to keep them from discolouring. Also keep them in water until the lamb is tender. Put them in the pan with the stems upwards. Add salt, and water if necessary.

When everything is ready, prepare the lemon sauce. Beat the eggs and add the lemon juice drop by drop, then 1-2 cups of the meat stock, beating this in slowly. Finally, pour this sauce into the pan with the meat and shake to distribute the sauce evenly.

lamb in the pot
(arní youvétsi me kritharáki)

1 portion, calories: 820.
Cooking time: 60 minutes.

portions: 5-6

1	kilo of lamb, top side
5	very ripe tomatoes
1/2	cup of oil or butter
1/2	kilo of barley-shaped pasta
	grated cheese
	salt
	pepper

Cut the lamb into serving portions, wash it and place it in a roasting tin or, even better, in an earthernware pot. Add salt and pepper and the skinned and crushed tomatoes, the oil and a little water and allow to bake in a moderate oven.

When the lamb is almost done, pour in 4 cups of hot water and add the pasta. Add salt and stir. Allow the meat to finish in a moderate oven, turning it once or twice.

To be served with grated cheese.

Variation: 1. The meat can be put into five or six individual earthernware pots and the pasta cooked separate.
2. Veal can be used instead of lamb.

grilled lamb chops
(païdákia arnísia)

1 portion (4 lamb chops), calories: 390.
Cooking time: 30 minutes.

portions: 4-5

1	*kilo of lamb chops*
1/2	*cup of oil*
2	*large lemons*
	rigani, salt, pepper

Mix the oil with the juice of one of the lemons and the rigani. Pour this mixture on to the lamb chops and mix them so that it coats the chops well. Cover the chops and allow them to stand in a cool place for about 2 hours. Using a charcoal grill or the grill of a cooker, cook them, turning frequently so that they cook evenly.

To be served with village salad and fried potatoes (chips).

lamb on the spit

see festival dishes . . . . p. 119

kokoretsi

see festival dishes . . . . p. 120

kontosouvli

see festival dishes . . . . p. 123

sucking pig

see festival dishes . . . . p. 128

country lamb

see local specialities . . . . p. 132

Mince

Mince has all the goodness and all the versatility of the meat from which it is made, and a wide range of dishes are based on it. Meat of all kinds can, of course, be minced, but when we talk of 'mince' it is usually minced beef that we are thinking of. Minced beef is sold in a number of different qualities, but good mince is important. It should not contain unsuitable parts of the carcase (gristle, skin) and it should not be too fatty; if it is, the fat will run off during cooking and will make it difficult to calculate the quantities of ingredients the dish requires.

One particular feature of Greek mince-based dishes is that they often provide good combinations of animal proteins with the proteins and vitamins found in vegetables. A portion of moussaka, for example, gives the body a small quantity of many different ingredients, as it contains mince, aubergines, eggs, milk, cheese, olive oil, and more.

The recipes in this chapter are among the most tasty of their kind. Perhaps among them you will find dishes become your favourites. A rosé wine is suitable for the dishes with white sauces and for grills (stuffed vine leaves, hamburgers), while the more highly-seasoned dishes, with tomato sauces ('soutzoukakia', moussaka) could be accompanied by either a light red wine or real Greek retsina.

grilled hamburgers.
(biftékia scáras)

1 large hamburger, calories: 350.
Cooking time: 20-30 minutes.

portions: 3-4

1/2   kilo of minced beef
1   egg
1/2   cup of crushed rusk bread
2   cloves of garlic, crushed
1   onion, finely chopped
      parsley, finely chopped
2   tablespoonfuls of oil
      lemon juice, salt, pepper

Mix the mince with the crushed rusk, the crushed garlic, the chopped onion and add the egg, the oil, parsley and the salt and pepper. Mix the ingredients well and then mould them into a round, flat shape. Grill them on both sides evenly and serve with lemon juice.

meat balls I
(keftédes I)

1 portion (4 normal-sized meatballs), calories: 440.
Cooking time: 15 minutes.

portions: 10-12

1   kilo of veal or beef mince
2   onions, finely chopped
250   grms of crustless bread soaked in water
3-4   teaspoonfuls of salt
2   eggs, 1 small bunch of parsley
      mint, pepper, a little flour

Squeeze as much water as possible from the bread. Combine it with the mince meat and the other ingredients. Chop the mint and the parsley finely and add the eggs. Knead the mixture so that all the ingredients are well combined. Allow the mixture to stand in the fridge for a while. Pour some oil into a frying pan and heat. Mould the meatballs, coat them with flour and fry them.

meat balls II (served as appetizers)
(keftédes II 'yia mezé')

1 portion (4 small meat balls), calories: 320.
Cooking time: 10-15 minutes.

portions: 12-14

1	kilo of veal or beef mince
250	grms of crustless bread soaked in water
2	eggs
2	onions, finely chopped
3	cloves of garlic, finely chopped
3-4	tablespoonfuls of ouzo
	rigani, salt, pepper
	a little flour

Mix all the ingredients as for meat balls, and knead the mixture while pouring the ouzo slowly into it. Allow to stand in the fridge for a short while, making sure it is covered with a clean cloth. Then, mould them into small balls and fry them.

Variation: Finely chopped pickles can be added to the sauce if wished.

meat balls, 'marinati'
(keftédes marináti)

1 portion (2 big meat balls), calories: 90.
Cooking time: 30-40 minutes.

portions: 8-10

500	grms of mince, not too lean
2	onions, grated
3	slices of crustless bread soaked in water
2	teaspoonfuls of salt
	a little pepper and rigani
1	cup of oil
	vinegar
3	tablespoonfuls of flour
1/2	cup of water or meat stock
1/2	cup of tomato juice
3	gloves of garlic, crushed
	red pepper
	parsley, finely chopped

Mix the mince with the onions, the soaked bread (squeezed dry), the salt, the vinegar and the rigani. Knead these ingredients and mould into big meat balls. Coat each one with flour and fry them, using the cup of oil mentioned in the ingredients. Then strain the oil from the frying pan, wash the pan and use 5 tablespoons of frying oil. Add the flour to this and stir till brown. Pour in the tomato juice, the water (or meat stock if used), the crushed garlic, 3 tablespoons of vinegar and some parsley. Allow the sauce to come to the boil and pour this over the meat balls.

mince roll
(roló apo kimá)

1 portion (1 large slice), calories: 300.
Cooking time: 40-50 minutes.

portions: 5-6

700	grms of mince
1	cup of crushed rusk
1	onion, finely chopped
	a small portion of celery, finely chopped
1/2	cup of butter
1	egg, beaten
	salt
	pepper
4	tablespoonfuls of dry white wine
2	cups of tomato juice
5	hard-boiled eggs

Mix the mince, the crushed rusk, the onion, the celery and the beaten egg. Add salt and pepper and knead it all well. Spread the mixture on greaseproof paper or aluminium foil. Shell the hard boiled eggs and place them in a row in the middle of the mixture and roll it over them with the help of the greaseproof paper or foil.

Put the butter in a shallow pan to heat well and then put the roll into it, being careful not to break it open. Turn it on all sides to brown. Pour in the tomato juice and add some salt. Cover the pan and allow the roll to stew.

To be served with rice, chips or mashed potatoes.

Variation: Cook the roll in the oven with the tomato juice, the butter from the browning of the roll and some water.

meat balls with egg and lemon sauce
(youvarlákia avgolémono)

1 portion (5 meatballs and stock), calories: 370.
Cooking time: 30 minutes.

portions: 6

500	*grms of mince*
1/2	*cup of butter*
1/4	*cup of rice*
1	*egg*
1	*onion, medium-sized, finely chopped*
	parsley, finely chopped
	salt, pepper

for the sauce:

2-3	*eggs*
2	*lemons*

Mix the ingredients in a bowl and knead well. Mould into balls. Half fill a saucepan with water and put in the butter. Add some salt to the water and put the meatballs in one by one. When they are cooked, prepare the egg and lemon sauce according to the recipe for this sauce.

moussaka
(moussakás)

1 portion, calories: 900.
Preparation time: 40 minutes.
Cooking time: 30 minutes.

for a large-sized baking tin

2	kilos of large round aubergines
1	kilo of mince
1/2	cup of oil
2	large onions
5	ripe tomatoes
1/2	cup of dry white wine
	salt, pepper
	grated kefalotiri cheese
	oil for frying
2-3	portions of white sauce (bechamel)

Peel, wash and cut the aubergines into large, thin slices. Salt and leave them to drain. Prepare the mince by browning it with the oil and onion, which should be finely chopped. Stop the browning precess by pouring in the wine. Add the tomatoes, skinned and finely chopped, the salt and the pepper and allow to boil till all the moisture has been absorbed. Pour the oil into a frying pan and fry the aubergines. Then spread them in a large roasting tin and sprinkle with grated cheese. After the first layer, spread the mince on top and then add another layer of fried aubergines. Then sprinkle again with the grated cheese and pour on the white sauce, so that the surface of the moussaka is covered with a thick layer of sauce. Finally, sprinkle some more cheese over this so that the surface becomes crisp.

Variations: 1. For easier serving and firmer portions, a layer of potatoes can be used. These should have been cut into slices like the aubergines and fried in the same manner.

2. Moussaka with courgettes
This is made by keeping the same quantities as above and using the same ingredients, but replacing the aubergines with courgettes cut into slices and fried, to be spread in the same manner in the roasting tin.

1 portion, calories: 750.

stuffed cabbage leaves
(lahanodolmádes)

1 portion (3 large rolls), calories: 380.
Cooking time: 40-50 minutes.

portions: 8

1	*large cabbage*
1/2	*kilo of mince*
1/2	*cup of rice*
1	*onion, finely chopped*
	salt
	pepper
1	*cup of butter*
2 1/2	*tablespoonfuls of flour*
3	*eggs*
2	*lemons*

Bring a large saucepan of water to the boil with a little salt. Meanwhile, remove the outer leaves and the hard stalk from the cabbage. Wash it and put it into the boiling water and let it boil for ten minutes.

Mix the mince with the rice, salt, pepper and knead together well.

Take each leaf separately and put on each one a tablespoonful of the mince mixture. Fold the two ends of the leaf inwards and roll it up into a long narrow shape.

Place some spare cabbage leaves on the bottom of the pan, then put the stuffed cabbage leaves in concentric circles. Place a heavy plate on top of them to prevent them from breaking open during the process of cooking. Pour water to cover them in and boil them for 60-80 minutes.

When they are cooked, put them on a flat dish and prepare the sauce.

Put the rest of the butter to melt, add the flour and stir with a wooden spoon. Add some stock from the cooked leaves, stirring all the time, and beat in the eggs with the lemon juice. Take the sauce off the heat.

The cabbage rolls can then be served with the sharp white sauce poured over them.

small stuffed vine leaves with sharp sauce
(dolmadákia me xiní sáltsa)

1 portion (5 dolmades with sauce), calories: 360.
Cooking time: 40-50 minutes.

portions: 8

1/2	*kilo of mince*
1/4	*kilo of vine leaves*
1/2	*cup of rice*
1	*onion, finely chopped*
	parsley, finely chopped
1/2	*cup of butter*
	salt, pepper
1	*portion of sharp white sauce*

Scald the vine leaves for 5 minutes if they are fresh. If tinned vine leaves are used, wash them with warm water. If you feel they are not tender enough, they too can be scalded for 3 minutes. Make a mixture with the mince, the rice, the finely chopped onion, the parsley and the salt and pepper. Take the vine leaves one by one, put on one end of each one a spoonful of the mixture and roll them into a longish shape. Put them in concentric circles and on top of each other in a pan. Put in the butter and put a plate on top of them to hold them down and so that they don't open while boiling. Add enough water to cover them. Boil them on a moderate heat.

To be served with a sharp white sauce.

Variation: Sauce with lemon juice and eggs can be used instead of the sharp white sauce, according to the recipe in the chapter on sauces.

macaroni pie
(pastítsio)

1 portion (1 normal slice), calories: 700.
Cooking time: 30-40 minutes.

for a large-sized baking tin

1   kilo of macaroni
1   kilo of mince
2   large onions, finely chopped
2   cups of mashed tomatoes
1/2 cup of oil
1/2 cup of butter (for the macaroni)
    salt, pepper
10 cups of milk
1   cup of butter
1   cup of flour
8   eggs
3   cups of grated cheese

Put in frying pan the mince and the chopped onion and a minimum of water. Cook till water is absorbed, stirring once or twice. Pour the oil in and brown the mince. Add salt and pepper. Put in the tomatoes and allow the ingredients to boil on a low heat. Boil water in a big saucepan, add salt and put in the macaroni. When boiled, drain and spread half of it in a baking pan. Sprinkle with grated cheese and spread over it an even layer of the mince mixture. Spread on the rest of the macaroni, sprinkled with cheese and pour over it half of the cup of melted butter.

Prepare the bechamel sauce in the following way: Put 1 cup of butter on to heat and when it is heated, add the flour and stir with a wooden spoon. Add the milk, stirring continuously to avoid lumps. A further precaution is that the milk should have been warmed beforehand. Then add the cheese (keeping aside 2 tablespoonfuls) and a little salt. As soon as the sauce thickens, beat the eggs well and add them slowly to the sauce.

Pour the sauce over the contents of the baking pan, spreading it evenly and sprinkle it with the 2 tablespoonfuls of cheese that has been kept back. This will make the crust of

spaghetti with mince
(makarónia me kimá)

1 portion, calories: 680.

portions: 4-5

1/2 kilo of spaghetti
300 grms of mince
1/2 cup of oil
1/2 cup of butter
1   onion, finely chopped
2-3 ripe tomatoes; salt
    grated cheese for the spaghetti

Prepare the sauce with the mince as follows: Put in a saucepan the onion and the mince and combine together well. Heat, and once its own moisture has been absorbed, add the oil. As the mince cooks, add the tomatoes, which should have been skinned and crushed beforehand. Add salt, pepper and one cup of water. Allow to simmer till a thick sauce forms.

Now put plenty of water in another saucepan, adding salt. Once water has boiled, add the spaghetti, giving it a good stir. As soon as the pasta has softened, drain and add the butter. Serve with grated cheese sprinkled liberally over the spaghetti, then add the mince over this.

the sauce crisp. Bake in a moderate oven for 30-40 minutes until it has browned.

The ingredients for this recipe are suitable for a large baking tin, for cooking in an electric oven.

hamburgers in the oven with potatoes
(biftékia foúrnou me patátes)

1 portion (2 medium-sized hamburgers
with 7-8 potatoes), calories: 500.
Cooking time: 60 minutes.

portions: 3-4

1/2   kilo of minced beef
1   egg
1/2   cup of crushed rusk
1/2   cup of grated cheese
1   tablespoonful of butter
3   tablespoonfuls of milk
      rigani, salt and pepper
1/2   cup of oil
2   lemons
1   kilo of potatoes

Mix the mince with the egg, the crushed
rusk, the cheese, the butter, the milk and
add the rigani, salt and pepper. Knead the
mixture well and form into hamburgers.

Peel and wash the potatoes, then cut
them into cubes, spreading them in a
roasting pan. Sprinkle with salt, pepper and
some rigani. Then pour the lemon juice over
them. Place the hamburgers in the middle of
the pan in a row and pour oil over them.
Add 1-2 cups of water.

Cook for about an hour, turning them
over once one side has browned and is
cooked.

souzoukakia
(soutzoukákia)

1 portion (4 pieces), calories: 420.
Frying time: 15 minutes.
Cooking time: 10-15 minutes.

portions: 10

1	kilo of mince
5	cloves of garlic, crushed
1	teaspoons of cumin
1/4	cup of dry white wine
1	cup of soaked crustless bread
1	egg
	salt, pepper
1/4	cup of oil
	flour and oil for frying

ingredients for the sauce

1 ½	cups of skinned, mashed tomatoes
3	cups of water
1	teaspoonful of butter
	salt, pepper
	cinnamon and allspice

Put all the ingredients into a bowl and knead well. Mould mixture into small rolls of a longish shape and coat them with flour. Heat the oil and fry them. Meanwhile prepare the sauce. Boil on a low heat all the ingredients of the sauce. Before it thickens, put the little fried rolls in it and allow them to boil on a low heat for about 10-15 minutes.

aubergine slippers
(melitzánes papoutsákia)

1 portion (2 whole aubergines), calories: 110.
Cooking time: 60 minutes.

portions: 8

1 ½   *kilos of aubergines, medium-sized*
      and round
1   *large onion, finely chopped*
1   *cup of oil*
1/2   *kilo of mince*
      salt, pepper
1/2   *cup of dry white wine*
      parsley, finely chopped
      thick white sauce (bechamel)
      see page 48
2   *tablespoonfuls of grated cheese*

Remove the stems of the aubergines and wash them well. Cut them in half lengthwise and nick the insides. Coat them with oil, put them in a greased baking tin and allow to bake in the oven until quite soft. Put the oil in a pan and heat. Add the onion and allow to soften, then add the mince, the salt, the pepper, the wine and the finely chopped parsley. Allow this mixture to cook on a low heat for 30 minutes. Spread the aubergines with this mixture and cover it with 1 tablespoonful of the white sauce for each half aubergine. Finally, sprinkle with the grated cheese and bake for 30 minutes in a moderate oven.

One cup of tomato juice and 4 tablespoonfuls of oil may be added to the baking tin if it is wished to creake a sauce for the dish.

Variation: The aubergines can be fried instead of baked (before filling) if wished. In this case, there is no need to put oil in the tomato sauce.

stuffed courgettes
(kolokithákia yemistá)

1 portion (2 courgettes), calories: 400.
Cooking time: 40-45 minutes.

portions: 6

1 ½   kilo of large courgettes
3/4   of a kilo of mince
1/2   cup of rice
1/2   cup of butter
2   medium-sized onions, finely chopped
       parsley, salt and pepper
       egg and lemon sauce or sharp white
       sauce (see 'sauces', page 48)

Clean, scrape and wash the courgettes. Cut a small slice from along one side and empty them by hollowing out with a spoon or special scooper. Knead the mince meat with the rice, the finely chopped onions, the parsley, also finely chopped, and the salt and pepper. Fill the courgettes with this mixture. Do not fill them up completely but leave enough room for the swelling of the rice. Put them upright in a saucepan and add water until they are almost covered, then add the butter. Use the resultant stock (juice) for the egg and lemon sauce or the sharp white sauce following the recipes on page 48.

tomatoes stuffed with mince
(tomátes yemistés me kimá)

1 portion (2 medium tomatoes), calories: 820.
Cooking time: 50-60 minutes.

portions: 5

10   tomatoes
1/2   kilo of mince
1   medium-sized onion, finely chopped
1   cup of butter
1   cup of grated kefalograviera cheese
1   cup of rice, salt, pepper, nutmeg

Open the tomatoes by cutting a slice horizontally from the top (to be kept). Scoop out the tomatoes with a spoon, salt them and then drain. Put some butter in a frying pan with the finely chopped onion and fry until soft. Add the mince and the pulp of the tomatoes finely cut up and without the seeds; add the salt, the pepper, the rice and the nutmeg. Fill the tomatoes with this mixture and put back on their 'lids', which have been kept aside, and pour the rest of the butter over them. To be baked in a moderate oven for 50-60 minutes.

Variation: 1 cup of crushed rusk may be used instead of the rice.

Fish - Seafood

Above all, Greece means the sea. The Greek seas seethe with the most delicious fish and seafood, a whole world of delights taken from the depths to grace our tables. Fish is healthy and easily digestible, and as well as containing all the nutritive ingredients found in the animal kingdom is also rich in iodine, potassium phosphate, magnesium, calcium and vitamins A and D. The wide range of different kinds of fish are cooked in a host of ways to create a variety of tempting tastes. Thanks to these variations, fish can appear on the menu almost daily without ever over-staying its welcome.

In Greece, fish are divided into a number of categories depending on their quality —a matter of their taste, their place of origin and their freshness. The fish in the highest category are those generally held to be the tastiest: red mullet, sea bream, and a few others. These have white flesh and very little fat, while others, such as tuna, mackerel and sardines, have darker flesh and more fat, which puts them in a lower category. However, the nutritive value of fish does not vary from category to category, and what is most important of all is that they should be fresh and properly cooked. Fresh fish must be firm, with red gills and shiny eyes — and above all they must smell of the sea!

For fish and seafood dishes, we suggest a dry white wine with a delicate bouquet. More highly-spiced dishes, such as fish 'à la Spetsiota' or octopus with macaroni, could be served either with a mild rosé or with retsina.

fried salt cod
(bakaliáros pastós tiganitós)

1 portion (2 pieces), calories: 280.
Cooking time: 15 minutes.

portions: 4

1/2	kilo of salted cod
1	cup of flour
1	cup of water
1	egg
	a little salt
	oil for frying

Cut the cod into small slices and leave it in water overnight. Change the water once or twice. Then wash it in warm water, removing the skin and bones. Make a batter by beating the flour and water lightly with the egg and salt until it becomes a smooth paste. Put plenty of oil into a frying pan and when it is well heated, dip each piece of cod in this batter before frying in the pan.

To be served with garlic sauce.

fried sole
(glósses tiganités)

1 portion, calories: 290.
Cooking time: 15 minutes.

portions: 5

5	soles of average size
2	eggs
1	cup of flour
1/2	cup of butter
	salt, pepper
	parsley, finely chopped, lemon

Clean and wash the soles and remove the skin, nicking it at the end of the tail and pulling the skin towards the head. Salt and pepper them. Beat the eggs well and put the butter in a frying pan to heat till very hot. Dip the fish into the beaten egg and one by one, coat them with flour and fry until they are lightly browned on both sides.

To be served with the finely chopped parsley and lemon slices.

fried red mullet
(barboúnia tiganitá)

1 portion, calories: 300.
Cooking time: 15 minutes.

portions: 4

1	kilo of red mullet
1	cup of oil
2	lemons
	flour for frying
	salt

Clean the fish carefully, removing the gills, innards and scales. Salt and allow to stand. In the meantime, heat the oil to a high temperature. Flour the fish and place in the hot oil to fry till browned. Turn the fish over to brown evenly on the other side.

Serve with freshly cut slices of lemon and sprinkle with lemon juice too.

fried whitebait (small fry)
(marídes tiganités)

1 portion, calories: 330.
Cooking time: 15-20 minutes.

portions: 4

1/2	kilo of medium-sized whitebait
1/2	cup of flour
	salt, pepper and lemon
	oil for frying

Wash the whitebait without gutting them and leave to stand for a while.

Put a generous amount of oil into a deep frying pan. Coat the whitebait with flour, shaking them to remove any surplus, then place them in the hot oil to fry. The oil, it must be stressed, must be at boiling point. When the fish is brown, it is ready to serve.

To be served with freshly milled pepper and garnished with slices of lemon.

grilled bream
(lithrínia sti scára)

1 portion (2 fish), calories: 340.
Cooking time: 30 minutes.

portions: 2-3

1   kilo of bream
1/2 cup of oil
2   lemons
     parsley, finely chopped
     salt
     rigani

Clean, wash and salt the bream. Coat it with oil and broil it on a well heated grill. Turn it to cook evenly and coat with oil at each turn. When it has grilled, place it on a flat dish.

Prepare the oil and lemon, add the parsley and the rigani, pour it over the fish and serve on a flat plate.

fish 'marinata'
(psária marináta)

1 portion, calories: 480.
Cooking time: 15 + 15 minutes.

portions: 3-4

1   kilo of fish
1/2 cup of vinegar
1/2 cup of dry white wine
1   cup of oil
1   cup of water, 3 tablespoonfuls of flour
     rosemary, salt, pepper

Clean the fish, salt them and fry them in the usual manner. Prepare the sauce in the following manner: In a frying pan, heat the oil well, put in the flour and stir. Add the wine, the vinegar, the salt, the pepper and the rosemary. Supplement with water and allow the sauce to thicken. Allow the fish to boil for a short while in this sauce and then serve.

fish à la spetsiota
(psári ala spetsióta)

1 portion, calories: 460.
Cooking time: 40-50 minutes.

portions: 6

1 ½   kilos of firm-fleshed-fish (gurnard,
      pike or striped bass)
1   cup of oil
1/2   kilo of onions, sliced
1 ½   cups of tomato juice
1   cup of white wine
1   cup of crushed rusk
1/2   kilo of sliced tomatoes
2-3   cloves of garlic
      parsley, finely chopped
      salt, pepper
      a little sugar

Wash the fish and cut in into slices. Salt it lightly and drain it. Coat a baking tin with oil. Place the pieces of fish in the baking tin and cover them with the slices of onion. Add salt and pepper and sprinkle the wine over each piece of fish. Make a mixture with the oil and the tomato juice, the sugar and salt and pepper. Blend together well, then pour half of it over the fish. Then mix the crushed rusk with the sliced garlic and finely chopped parsley and spread this mixture over the fish. Then spread the tomato slices lay the fish on. Finally, pour the rest of the tomato sauce mixture over it. Allow to bake in a moderate oven for about 40-50 minutes.

octopus stew with onions
(htapódi stifádo)

1 portion, calories: 460.
Cooking time: 50-60 minutes.

portions: 8-10

2	kilos of octopus
1 ½	kilos of small onions
6	cloves of garlic, finely chopped
8-10	whole peppercorns
1	large tin of skinned tomatoes
2	cups of oil
1/2	cup of red wine
1/2	cup of vinegar
	bay leaves, salt

Cut the octopus into pieces, wash them and put them into a saucepan without water. Cook until its moisture has been absorbed, then add the vinegar. Also add the oil and stir with a wooden spoon. Then put in the onions and the finely chopped garlic, the wine and the mashed tomatoes and, finally, the peppercorns and the bay leaves. Add salt and allow to boil on a moderate heat, frequently stirring to avoid sticking.

stuffed squid
(kalamarákia yemistá)

1 portion (2 medium-sized squid), calories: 600.
Cooking time: 45 minutes.

portions: 5-6

1 ½	kilos of large squid
1	cup of rice
1	cup of finely chopped spring onions
1	cup of oil
1	small bunch of dill, finely chopped
	salt, pepper

Clean the squid and remove the bone, the eyes and the hard parts and then wash them well. Cut the tentacles into small pieces and put them into a frying pan with the finely chopped onions to fry. When the moisture has been absorbed, add threequarters of a cup of oil and salt and pepper. Stir this mixture with a spatula and add the rice, constantly stirring to avoid sticking. Pour in a half a cup of water and add the dill and allow these ingredients to boil gently for a little while until all moisture has been absorbed

and only the oil remains. Stuff the body of the squid with this mixture and leave enough room in each to allow the rice to swell. Then with a needle and clean thread sew up each squid carefully and place them in a shallow pan. Pour in the rest of the oil and enough water to cover them to the middle. Allow to boil for 45 minutes until all the water has been absorbed.

octopus with macaroni
(htapódi me makaronáki koftó)

1 portion (205 grms), calories: 580.
Cooking time: 60 minutes.

portions: 5-6

1   *kilo octopus*
1/2 *kilo of short macaroni*
1/2 *kilo of fresh, ripe tomatoes*
1   *cup of wine*
1 ½ *cups of oil*
1   *large onion, finely chopped*
    salt
    pepper

Cut the octopus into medium-sized pieces and wash well. Put them into a saucepan and boil till all the moisture has been absorbed. Then add the finely chopped onion and the oil and allow the onion to soften, stirring with a wooden spatula. Add the wine and the skinned and crushed tomatoes. Add salt and pepper and a requisite amount of water to boil. When the octopus has softened, add some more water and the macaroni. Serve as soon as the macaroni is tender and the water has been absorbed.

cuttlefish with spinach
(soupiés me spanáki)

1 portion, calories: 440.
Cooking time: 40-50 minutes.

portions: 6-7

1	kilo of cuttlefish
1	kilo of spinach
1	cup of oil
1/4	cup of white wine
4-5	spring onions
1	small bunch of dill
	mint
	salt
	pepper

Clean the cuttlefish, removing the bone and the ink. Pour the ink into a small basin and add 3 cups of water and allow it to settle. Pour the oil into a pan to heat, adding the finely chopped onions, the dill and the mint. Then add the cuttlefish after having cut it into small pieces. Salt them lightly and pepper them. Pour off as much water as you can from the ink mixture without disturing the sediment.

Pour a little water with the ink into the pan and boil. When the cuttlefish is almost ready, add the spinach thickly cut. Add now and again some of the mixture of water and ink till the fish is well boiled. When it is ready, take off boil by pouring in the white wine.

cuttlefish with rice
(soupiés piláfi)

1 portion, calories: 540.
Cooking time: 40-50 minutes.

portions: 6-7

1	kilo of cuttlefish
1	cup of oil
1 1/2	cups of tomato juice
2	cups of rice
2	onions, finely chopped
	salt, pepper

Remove the small sacs of ink carefully and dissolve it with water in a basin. Cut the cuttlefish into pieces and wash these well. Brown the finely chopped onions in the oil and add the cuttlefish. Pour in the tomato juice, add the salt and the pepper and allow to boil for 1 hour approximately. Then pour the solution of ink into the pot, with additional water. As soon as this boils, add the rice. Lower the heat and allow to boil until cuttlefish is tender and the rice is soft.

cuttlefish yiahni
(soupiés yiahní)

1 portion, calories: 430.
Cooking time: 40-50 minutes.

portions: 6

1	kilo of cuttlefish
1	cup of oil
1	cup of dry white wine
1 1/2	cups of tomato juice
1	large onion, finely chopped
	salt, pepper

Clean the cuttlefish, removing the bone and innards. Cut into pieces. Put the oil and the finely chopped onion in a pan to soften and add the cuttlefish. Add salt and pepper and after stirring them for a while, add the wine. Complete with tomato juice and add as much water as necessary until fish is tender.

shrimps in the pot
(garídes ýouvetsáki)

1 portion, calories: 490.
Cooking time: 30-40 minutes.

portions: 6

1	kilo of large shrimps
300	grms of feta cheese
2	cups of oil
1	large tin of skinned tomatoes
1	small bunch of parsley
2	onions, finely chopped
	rigani, salt, pepper

Put in a frying pan the oil and the finely chopped onions and fry till softened. Add the tomatoes, slightly mashed with a fork, then add the salt and pepper and allow this sauce to boil for a while.

Clean and wash the shrimps and divide them into six individual portions, putting them into six earthernware pots. Also divide the sauce and allot a sixth of it to each pot. Then sprinkle all the pots with the finely chopped parsley and rigani. Cut the feta into largish chunks and put one chunk into each of the pots on top of the shrimps. Allow to bake in a moderate oven for about 30-40 minutes.

shrimps with rice
(garídes piláfi)

1 portion, calories: 570.
Cooking time: 30 minutes approximately.

portions: 6

1	kilo of shrimps (or prawns)
2 ½	cups of rice
1	cup of oil
1 ½	cups of tomato juice (or small tomatoes, skinned and crushed)
1	onion, large and finely chopped
	salt
	pepper

Remove the whiskers from the shrimps and wash well (the shrimps not the whiskers). Salt them and allow to drain. Heat the oil and put in the finely chopped onions. As soon as the onions have softened, add the tomato juice, the salt and the pepper. Allow the sauce to boil for about 10-15 minutes. Then add 2-3 cups of water and the rice. When the rice is almost boiling, add the shrimps. Allow to boil together for about 15 minutes until the water has been absorbed and according to your preference as to the softness of the rice.

To be served hot.

boiled salt cod
(bakaliáros vrastós)

1 portion, calories: 340.
Cooking time: 30-40 minutes.

portions: 5-6

1	kilo of cod
6	potatoes
6	carrots
3	onions
1/2	cup of oil
2	lemons
	salt

Put the cod in water to soak overnight, changing the water once or twice.

The skin and bones can be removed, if wished. Put the vegetables into a saucepan of water with the oil and allow to cook. When they are almost tender, add the cod. When it is finally ready, pour the lemon juice into the saucepan.

With each portion serve some juice and a portion of vegetables.

boiled lobster with oil and lemon sauce
(astakós vrastós me sáltsa lemonioú)

1 portion, calories: 260.
Cooking time: 40-50 minutes.

portions: 4-6

1	large, fresh lobster
1	stick of celery
1	cup of oil
2	large lemons
	salt
	white pepper

Wash the lobster and stop up the little hole at the end of his tail with a piece of cotton to avoid the emptying of the shell. Do the same to any broken claw. If the saucepan is not large enough, tie the lobster with string, fastening the tail to the middle. Put water in the saucepan — if at all possible, sea water is preferable, otherwise add salt. Allow to boil for 40-50 minutes. Then remove from heat and drain. When the lobster has cooled, cut off the claws and remove the shell very carefully. Cut the flesh lengthwise and remove the intestinal cord which is situated at its centre. Collect the eggs and the lobster brains with a spoon and set aside. Remove the flesh from the claws. Cut all the lean meat into slices and spread on a large, flat dish.

Prepare a well-beaten sauce with the oil, the lemon juice, the white pepper and the lobster eggs and brains. Then pour this sauce over the lobster.

boiled fish with vegetables
(psári vrastó me lachaniká)

1 portion (with vegetables), calories: 350.
Cooking time: 40 minutes.

portions: 4-5

1	*fish sea (gurnard, pike or sea bream)*
	1 kilo approximately
8	*medium-sized potatoes*
6	*carrots*
3	*onions*
2	*tomatoes*
2	*sticks of celery*
1/2	*cup of oil*
	salt
	pepper

Peel and wash the potatoes, the onions, the carrots and the celery and put them in a saucepan to boil whole with plenty of water. Add the oil, the tomatoes, cut into four parts, and a little salt. Remove the scales, the innards and the gills of the fish. Salt it and allow it to stand for a while.

When the vegetables are almost ready, add the fish to them and allow to boil together. Drain the fish and serve it in a oval dish, garnishing it by placing the vegetables around it attractively. The juice can be strained and served with lemon or can be made into a delicious soup.

cod salmi
(bakaliáros plakí)

1 portion, calories: 285.
Cooking time: 60 minutes.

portions: 6

1	*flat salt cod (600-700 grms)*
1 ½	*kilos of potatoes*
4	*cloves of garlic*
1 ½	*cups of tomato juice*
	rigani, parsley, finely chopped
1 ½	*cups of oil*
	salt, pepper

Cut the cod into pieces and leave in water overnight. Wash it with warm water; remove the skin and bones. Cut the potatoes into slices, having washed them well first, and spread them in a baking tin, sprinkling them with the finely chopped parsley and salt and pepper. Place the cod on the potatoes and add the garlic, the rigani and more parsley and pepper. Then one more layer of potatoes is spread on top, with the addition again of garlic, rigani, parsley, salt and pepper. To be completed by sprinkling tomato juice and oil all over the surface.

small fry
(gávros plakí)

1 portion, calories: 330.
Cooking time: 40-50 minutes.

portions: 3-4

1/2	*kilo of small fry*
1/2	*cup of oil*
2	*ripe tomatoes*
1	*small bunch of parsley*
	garlic
	salt, pepper

Wash the fish well, removing the heads, tails and innards. Place them (the fish) in a baking tin; salt and pepper them. Wash the tomatoes and crush them. Finely chop the garlic and the parsley and add to the fish in the baking tin. Also add the tomatoes and the oil, along with 1 cup of water. Cook the fish for about 40-50 minutes in a moderate oven.

Variation: The small fry can be baked with oil and rigani. In this case, you omit the other ingredients and substitute oil, the juice of 2 lemons and rigani.

sea pike with oil and rigani
(zargánes ladorígani)

1 portion, calories: 360.
Cooking time: 40 minutes.

portions: 6-7

1	kilo of sea pike
1	cup of oil
2	lemons
	rigani
	salt
	pepper

Clean the fish well, removing innards and cutting off the snout. Because this fish is long, it should be cut in two. Place the fish in a baking tin, salt and pepper it ; coat with plenty of lemon juice and sprinkle liberally with rigani. Then, add the oil with one cup of water.

Cook in a moderate oven for 40 minutes.

sliced fish with oil and rigani in the oven
(psári féta sto foúrno ladorígani)

1 portion, calories: 460.
Cooking time: 60 minutes.

portions: 4-6

1	kilo of firm fish (gurnard, pike or tunny fish)
1	kilo of potatoes
1 ½	cups of oil
2	lemons
	salt, pepper and rigani

Clean the fish and cut into slices. Peel the potatoes and cut them into long narrow slices. Place the fish in the middle of the baking tin along with the potatoes arranged around it. Salt and pepper and sprinkle with rigani. Add the oil, the juice of the lemons and one and a half cups of water. Allow to bake in a moderate oven for about 1 hour.

stuffed mussels
(mídia yemistá)

1 portion (5 mussels), calories: 350.
Cooking time: 30 minutes.

portions: 8-10

1 ½	kilos of mussels
1 ½	cups of rice
1	cup of oil
2	medium-sized onions, finely chopped
2	tablespoons of pine nuts
	salt, pepper

Clean the mussels well and scrape shells with a wire brush to remove any weeds and foreign bodies. Put them in a saucepan with a minimum amount of water and put them on to heat. Once the mussels have opened, remove them from the heat, allowing them to cool, and prepare the stuffing. Put the finely chopped onions on to heat with half the oil and fry till soft and browned. Add the rice, the pine nuts and salt and pepper. Stir several times. As soon as the mixture browns lightly, remove from heat. Allow the stuffing to cool and begin to fill the already opened mussels with this mixture. Close the shells with their contents and place the mussels in a shallow pan. Add the rest of the oil and the water that remains from the opening of the shells in the other saucepan and allow to stew till cooked.
To be served cold.

boiled octopus

see appetizers p.10

swordfish kebabs
(xifías souvláki)

1 portion, calories: 230.
Cooking time: 20 minutes.

portions: 4-5

500	grms of swordfish
2	firm tomatoes
2	green peppers
2	onions
	salt, pepper
	rigani, oil

Cut the swordfish into cubes and do the same with the tomatoes, the peppers and the onions. Roll the ingredients in oil, rigani, salt and pepper. Thread the pieces of swordfish, the tomatoes, the peppers and the onions on to small skewers or wooden spits.
Roast them on the grill, catching the juices and pouring them back over the pieces.
Grill till tender and serve.

octopus in wine

see appetizers . . . . p. 10

fried mussels

see appetizers p.11

cod croquettes

see appetizers p.11

fish soup

see soups p.42

greek bouillabaise

see soups . . . . p. 42

Vegetables Ladera

Greece is a vegetarian's paradise. All year round the markets are crammed with high-quality vegetables of all kinds whose colour and freshness challenge one to dare walk past without buying! The unique combinations of soil conditions and the mild climate mean that Greek vegetables have a taste all their own. For that reason, vegetables in Greece are used not as a supplement to other types of food or as decoration on the plate but as complete dishes in themselves. The filling meals which can be produced just from vegetables are a delight to vegetarians and also to those who like a little variety in their daily menu.

Greek cuisine has a wide range of dishes using only vegetables. All of them are based on olive oil, which is what their Greek name means. Beans, okra, aubergines, courgettes, peppers, artichokes: when cooked with oil and spices these produce tasty and attractive dishes. Vegetable dishes are often accompanied by feta cheese, whose slightly salty taste sets them off to perfection.

artichokes with broad beans
(angináres me koukiá)

1 portion, calories: 370.
Cooking time: 90 minutes.

portions: 6

1	kilo of fresh broad beans
6	artichokes
1 ½	cups of oil
5	small, spring onions, cut into fine slices
1	small bunch of dill, finely chopped
2	lemons
	salt, pepper

Shell the beans and throw away the tough and damaged ones. Wash them well.

Take each artichoke and break off the tough outer leaves, then slice off the stalk and trim the base. Snip off the leaves then, using a spoon or scoop, scrape out the hairy insides. Rub with lemon juice and allow the hearts to stand in water so they don't blacken.

Then put the onions and oil into a pan and cook till softened. Add the dill and lemon juice. Add to this 2 cups of water and then add the beans and the artichokes. Salt and pepper the ingredients and allow to boil on a moderate heat for about one and half hours.

artichokes à la polita
(angináres alá políta)

1 portion, calories: 340.
Cooking time: 90 minutes.

portions: 4

8	artichokes
3	lemons
6	small spring onions
10	large onions
1/2	kilo of small potatoes
1	small bunch of dill, finely chopped
1	cup of oil, salt, pepper

Break off the tough outer leaves of the artichoke and then slice off the stem. Trim the base and cut off the leaves and rub them in lemon juice. Allow them to stand in water. Finely slice the spring onions and cut the other onions into four. Put them into a saucepan with the artichokes and the potatoes. Add the oil, the dill, the salt and the pepper and plenty of water to cover. Allow to cook for about an hour and a half until all the water has been absorbed and only the oil remains.

Variation: If wished, 3 finely sliced carrots can also be added.

artichokes with egg and lemon and peas
(angináres me araká avgolémono)

1 portion, calories: 385.
Cooking time: 60 minutes.

portions: 4

8	artichokes
1/2	kilo of peas
6-8	small spring onions
1	small bunch of dill, finely chopped
1	cup of oil
2	eggs
2	small lemons, salt, pepper

Break off the tough outer leaves of the artichokes, then slice off the soft leaves and scrape out the hairy centres. Rub them with lemon juice and allow them to stand in water. Cut the small onions into thin slices and put them in a saucepan to heat until softened. Put in the lemon juice and the dill and add the artichokes and the peas, which should have been well washed beforehand. Salt and pepper the ingredients, adding 2 cups of water; allow to cook for about 1 hour until only the oil remains, the water having been absorbed.

yellow pea purée
(fáva)

1 portion, calories: 390.
Cooking time: 65 minutes.

portions: 6-8

1/2	kilo of dried yellow peas
1	onion
1/2	cup of oil
	salt, pepper
	parsley, finely chopped
1	onion, finely chopped

Wash the peas and put them in a pan with lots of water, making sure the water covers the peas well. Heat to boil and remove the scum which forms, then add the onion cut in two. Allow to boil for about an hour on a low heat.

Then follow this by putting the pea and onion mixture through a vegetable mill. Put into a frying pan with half the oil, the salt, the pepper and cook, stirring, for approximately 5 minutes and then serve. Pour the rest of the oil on top and sprinkle with finely chopped onion and parsley.

aubergine 'imam'
(melitzánes imám)

1 portion, calories: 340.
Cooking time: 60 minutes.

portions: 6

6	aubergines, medium-sized, round
5	onions
10	cloves of garlic
5	ripe tomatoes, skinned and crushed
1	small bunch of parsley, finely chopped
2 1/2	cups of oil
	salt, pepper

Wash the aubergines well and remove the stems. Cut 3 slits lengthwise in each aubergine. Salt them. Put one and a half cups of oil into a frying pan and fry the aubergines on all sides evenly. Remove them and place them in a baking tin.

Pour into the frying pan the rest of the oil. Clean the onions and cut into thick slices. Wash the garlic and cut each clove into 3-4 pieces. Put the garlic and the onion into the frying pan and fry. Once they have softened, add the tomatoes, the parsley, the salt and the pepper. Allow the ingredients to fry for a while, then fill the aubergines with the mixture through the slits that have been made earlier. Empty the contents of the frying pan into the baking tin and then add one and a half cups of water.

Bake in the oven for about 1 hour.

aubergines with potatoes
(melitzánes me patátes katsarólas)

1 portion, calories: 320.
Cooking time: 40 minutes.

portions: 4-6

1   kilo of potatoes
1   kilo of aubergines, large and long
      in shape
2   onions, finely chopped
4   ripe tomatoes, crushed
1   small bunch of parsley, finely chopped
1 ½   cups of oil
      salt, pepper

Clean and wash the potatoes and dice them, leaving them in water. Clean and wash the aubergines, remove the stems and cut into thick slices (3-5 slices each, depen-ding on the size), salt them well and let them drain. Put the onion with the oil to heat in a frying pan. Once the onion has softened, add the washed and crushed tomatoes, salt and pepper and the parsley. Bring to the boil and simmer for a minute or two. Then add the potatoes and the aubergines. Mix well.

Add 3-4 cups of water. Cover the pan and allow to simmer until all the moisture has been absorbed and you have a sauce.

Variation: If wished, instead of the aubergines, courgettes can be used; or courgettes can also be used with the aubergines and potatoes but the amounts of each would have to be reduced.

oven roasted potatoes
(patátes foúrnou ladorígani)

1 portion, calories: 400.
Cooking time: 60 minutes.

portions: 6

1 ½   kilos of medium-sized potates
1   cup of oil
2   lemons, rigani, salt, pepper

Wash the potatoes well and cut them lengthwise; place them in a roasting tin. Sprinkle with salt and pepper, rigani and the juice from the 2 lemons and mix all the ingredients together well. Add the oil and 3 cups of water. Roast in the oven for approximately 1 hour.

'briam' baked potatoes with courgettes
(briám me patátes ke kolokithákia)

1 portion, calories: 270.
Cooking time: 60 minutes.

portions: 4-6

1	kilo of potatoes
1	kilo of medium-sized courgettes
1/2	kilo of fresh tomatoes
6	cloves of garlic, finely chopped
1	small bunch of parsley, finely chopped
1 ½	cups of oil
	salt
	pepper

Wash the potatoes and cut them into round slices. Clean and wash the courgettes and cut them lengthwise into slices. Spread one layer of potatoes in a medium-sized baking tin. Salt and pepper them. On top, spread a layer of courgettes and salt and pepper them too, then sprinkle on half of the chopped parsley. Spread 3 of the finely chopped garlic cloves on the courgettes. Skin the tomatoes, add some more courgettes with the pulp of the tomato and continue putting a layer in turn; potato then courgette, the parsley, the garlic and the tomato, making sure each layer is evenly spread. Then salt and pepper it all. Add the oil and 2-3 cups of water.

Bake in the oven for about 1 hour.

Variation: If wished, you can replace half of the courgettes with aubergines.

spinach with rice
(spanakórizo)

1 portion, calories: 240.
Cooking time: 45 minutes.

portions: 5-6

1	kilo of spinach
6	small spring onions
1	small bunch of dill, finely chopped
1 ½	cups of rice
1	cup of oil
	salt, pepper
	lemon

Wash the spinach as well as possible and cut as finely as you can. Drain well. Clean the onions and cut them into fine slices. Put them into a saucepan with the oil and cook till softened. Then add the dill and cook for a little while longer.

Add the spinach and stir it well for a short time, then add the salt and pepper. Add 3 cups of water and allow to boil.

After the spinach has almost cooked, add a further 3 cups of water and put in the rice. Cover the saucepan and allow all the ingredients to cook on a moderate heat, stirring occasionally.

When the water has been absorbed, serve with freshly ground pepper and lemon juice.

okra in oil
(bámies laderés)

1 portion, calories: 180.
Cooking time: 40 minutes.

portions: 3-4

1/2	kilo of okra
2	medium-sized onions
3	ripe tomatoes
1/2	cup of oil
	salt
	pepper
	vinegar

Wash the okra well. Remove the stems with a sharp knife. Put 1 soupspoonful of salt and 3 spoonfuls of vinegar on a plate and dip each okra head in this, then put them into a pan.

Clean the onions and cut them into fine slices and add them to the okra, along with the skinned and crushed tomatoes and the oil, the salt and pepper. Add to this 2 cups of water and allow to cook slowly. Ensure that the okra does not overcook and go mushy.

stuffed tomatoes and peppers
(tomátes ke piperiés yemistés)

1 portion (1 tomato and 1 pepper), calories: 420.
Cooking time: 60 minutes.

portions: 6

6	*firm ripe tomatoes*
6	*large green peppers*
2	*onions, finely chopped*
1	*cup of tomato juice*
1	*small bunch of parsley, finely chopped*
12	*soupspoonfuls of rice*
1 ½	*cups of oil*
	salt, pepper
	sugar

Wash the tomatoes and peppers very well. From one end of each tomato cut a slice (from the top end, usually), but be sure not to detach it completely as it must act as a lid. Then with a spoon empty the tomato of all the pulp, ensuring that you do not puncture the skin. From the pulp the seeds must be removed and disposed of. Then do the same to the peppers (operating from the end where the stem was). The seeds from the peppers are also to be disposed of. Then arrange the hollowed tomatoes and peppers in a baking tin.

Place the onion and one cup of oil in a frying pan. Before the onions have quite softened, add the rice and fry till transparent. Chop up the pulp of the tomatoes, add this to the juice and to the rice. Add salt and pepper and the finely chopped parsley, adding to the frying pan half a cup of water. Allow

the ingredients to cook till most of the water has been absorbed.

Reduce the heat and put in each hollowed out tomato and pepper half a teaspoonful of sugar. Then fill (each tomato and pepper) to half way with the rice mixture. Some room must be left for the swelling of the rice. Add one soupspoonful of water and a teaspoonful of sugar and close the lids. Pour the tomato juice into the baking tin with the other half cup of oil. Sprinkle with salt and pepper and bake for about 1 hour.

Variation: You can, if wished, add potatoes sliced lengthwise to the baking tin, placed between each tomato and pepper.

potatoes yiahni
(patátes yiahní)

1 portion, calories: 450.
Cooking time: 30 minutes.

portions: 6

1 ½	kilo of small round potatoes
1	large onion
3	ripe tomatoes
1	cup of oil
	salt
	pepper

Wash and clean the potatoes well. If they are quite small, leave them whole, but if larger, cut into two. Chop the onion finely and put it into a pan with the oil.

Then add the skinned and crushed tomatoes, the salt and the pepper and allow the mixture to boil well for a while, then add the potatoes. Mix it all up well and add 3 cups of water.

Allow to boil till you have a thick sauce.

green beans in oil
(fasolákia prásina laderá)

1 portion, calories: 370.
Cooking time: 30-40 minutes.

portions: 4

1	kilo of green beans
1	large onion
3	ripe tomatoes, skinned and crushed
1	cup of oil
	salt, pepper

If the beans are rounded, cut off both ends, but if you have bought flat beans, clean them and remove the stringy spine.

Wash them well and put them into a saucepan with the onion, which needs to be thinly sliced, and pour in half a cup of water. Cook to soften the onion and beans together. Pour in the oil and add the tomatoes, the salt and the pepper to the pan. Then add a further 2 cups of water and allow to cook till well boiled.

Variation: If wished, potatoes cut into large cubes also can be added. They must be put in with the beans already half cooked.

Festival Dishes

Every day is a feast day somewhere in Greece. The religious and folklore tradition is so strong that even if we wanted to, it would be impossible to list all the festival days.

In the cities and, principally, the rural areas there are picturesque local celebrations of great interest to visitors. We shall concentrate here on some feast days which are celebrated with enthusiasm all over the country and which, of course, are accompanied by special meals.

Carnival - 'Clean Monday'

Before Lent, the period of fasting and purification that leads to Easter, the Greek calendar contains three weeks of enjoyment and fun: Carnival time. During the Carnival there are dances and parties everywhere, with plenty of eating and drinking. The particular forms which celebrations take vary from one part of the country to another. They include the wearing of costumes, the presentation of amusing or daring performances, dancing and much consumption of wine and are reminiscent of the ancient worship of the god Dionysus. Sucking pig is the most characteristic Carnival dish. It can be spit-roasted, fried or stewed with spaghetti and cheese. However, all the spicy meat dishes and all those served as mezedes with wine are suitable for carnival time. What is really essential is plenty of wine and as much 'kefi' as possible!

The last Sunday of Carnival is followed by 'Clean Monday', the first day of Lent. Clean Monday acquired its name in olden times: it was the day on which the housewives cleaned all their kitchen utensils to get rid of the last traces of the Carnival food. Clean Monday is a preparation for Lent and old traditions are maintained. Family groups and friends head for the mountains or the seaside and spread their table with raw salads (lettuce, spring onions, radishes), seafood (mussels, crabs, prawns, oysters), olives, pickles, cod roe salad, halva and boiled beans and potatoes.

One of the centrepieces is the Clean Monday loaf, the 'lagana', which is only produced by the bakeries on this one day in the year. The lagana is long and flat, with rounded corners and lots of sesame seeds.

It is traditional for children to fly kites on Clean Monday. The groups of accompanying adults, however, may use the Clean Monday table as an excuse for 'kefi' reaching even greater heights than the kites!

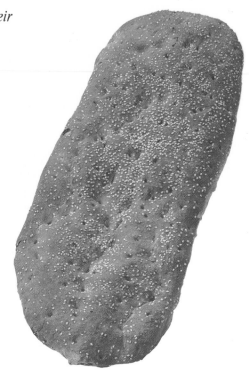

Easter

Greek Easter, the country's most important religious feast, arrives accompanied by the smells of spring, the rebirth of nature and the flower-carpeted ground.

The red eggs for just after the Resurrection and the traditional Resurrection soup, 'mayeiritsa', will be the housewife's first concern, and her preparations will begin early in Holy Week. That preparation means the cleaning and decoration of the house, the baking of Easter biscuits and bread and the dyeing of the eggs. All through Holy Week the churches are full each evening as people follow, once more, the Passion of Our Lord. Then at midnight on the Saturday the bells ring out joyfully; the faithful, candles lit, can celebrate the Resurrection. The meal afterwards consists of 'mayeiritsa'; the red eggs are 'knocked' and the traditional phrase "Christ is risen" will be heard all round the table.

On Easter Sunday, spit-roast lamb is the centrepiece of the table. From early in the morning the spits will be turning in courtyards and under shady trees as the lamb and its attendant 'kokoretsi' are slowly cooked, and the aroma of roasting meat wafts from one end of Greece to the other.

In the pages with follow, we have brought together for you the most delicious tastes of Greek Easter. Serve these dishes with plenty of green salads (particularly lettuce, which in Greece is in season at Easter) and red wine or retsina. If you get a chance to celebrate Greek Easter in Greece, don't pass it up; it will mean song, dance and 'kefi' around the fire-pit as the spit slowly revolves.

lamb on the spit
(arní soúvlas)

1 portion (without skin), calories: 315.
With skin, calories 380, approx.
Cooking time: approximately 3 hours.

1	lamb, 8-9 kilos
	butter, oil
	2-3 lemons
	salt
	pepper

Remove the intestines from the lamb. Wash it well and drain. Then salt and pepper the inside. Pass the spit carefully through it so that the backbone is parallel to it. Then tie it to the spit with thin wire or thick string so that it does not stir while cooking, then tie the legs securely to the spit, sewing up the stomach cavity with thick thread so it won't open during the cooking process. Baste the lamb well with butter and lemon juice and sprinkle liberally with salt and pepper.

Heat the charcoal and allow the fire to settle. Place the spit in position. Have close at hand a bowl with lemon juice and oil and a basting brush and once the rotation has started, baste often with this mixture. The rotation must be fast to begin with, but can be slowed down as the meat starts to cook. Keep basting with the lemon and oil to obtain a crisp skin.

kokoretsi
(kokorétsi)

1 portion, calories: 320.
Cooking time: 2-3 hours.

1	kilo livers
1	kilo lights
2	kilos of lambs' intestines
	fat of lamb
	salt, pepper, rigani

Wash the intestines well and turn inside out. Wash the offal and cut into pieces. Sprinkle liberally with salt and pepper and the rigani. Pass a roasting spit through the pieces of offal, alternating lights, liver and fat. Then tightly wrap all this with the intestines, tying with string to prevent it falling apart in the cooking process. Salt and pepper all the surface and allow to stand and drain for a couple of hours.

Roast over charcoal, or in an oven, making sure that it rotates rapidly to start with, then slows down to get it more evenly cooked.

easter soup
(mayirítsa)

1 portion, calories: 520.
Cooking time: 1 hour, 20 minutes.

portions: 8-9

1	kilo of lamb offal (liver, heart, lungs, etc)
1/2	kilo of spring onions
1	small bunch of dill
3/4	cup of rice
2	soupspoonfuls of butter the juice of 3 lemons
3	eggs salt, pepper

Bring the offal to the boil and remove the scum which forms on the surface. Salt it and allow to boil for a while, then remove from the water but keep the juice as stock. Cut the offal into very small pieces. Strain the stock from the offal into a large pan.

Chop the onion very finely, do the same to the dill and add them to the stock. Add the offal and the butter. Reduce heat and allow to simmer.

When it has thoroughly cooked, add the rice.

Prepare the egg and lemon. Beat the eggs well in a separate bowl and add the lemon juice drop by drop. Take a ladleful from the stock and add this to the egg and lemon mixture gradually. As the stock is added gradually, the mixture must be constantly beaten.

Add this mixture to the cooked offal and then serve with freshly ground pepper.

kontosouvli
(kontosoúvli)

1 portion, calories: 330.
Cooking time: 2-3 hours.

2	kilos of lamb or pork
2	soupspoonfuls of rigani salt, pepper; crushed onions

Cut the meat into small pieces (up to 30 grams each) and if you find any small bones, take them out.

Mix the meat with the onions, the rigani and the salt and the pepper. Cover the bowl and allow it to stand in the fridge overnight.

Pierce the portions of meat with a small spit and cook over charcoal embers.

easter cookies
(koulourákia paschaliná)

1 cooky, calories: 90.
Cooking time: 20 minutes.

1	kilo of flour
6	eggs
1	cup of clarified butter
	vanilla
2	small spoonfuls of powdered ammonia
300	grms of sugar
1/3	cup of milk
1	beaten egg (for glazing)

Put the flour in a bowl and make a well in the centre. Pour the butter (melted) into the well in the flour. When it has cooled, crumble the butter and flour with the fingers. Take the eggs and separate the yolks from the whites. Beat the yolks with sugar and beat the whites separately to make a meringue. Once again, form a well in the flour/butter mixture and add the yolk and sugar mixture, the meringue and the warmed milk, which has been mixed with the ammonia. Add the vanilla and knead all the ingredients well until you have a manageable dough. Mould the cookies into different shapes, placing them on a baking tray with a small distance between them, as they will swell when cooking. Coat with the beaten egg and bake in a moderate oven for 20 minutes.

easter bread
(tsourékia)

1 large slice, calories: 200.
Cooking time: 45 minutes.

1 ½ kilos of flour
400 grms of sugar
320 grms of butter
100 grms of yeast
230 grms of milk
8   eggs
1   teaspoonful of mastic, crushed
1/2 teaspoonful of mahlepi (an oriental
     seed-type herb)
     almonds blanched, browned
     and coarsely crushed

Dissolve the yeast in a little warm milk and add 3-4 tablespoons of flour. Leave the yeast to rise in a warm place. When it has risen sufficiently, put the rest of the flour into a bowl and make a well in the centre. Put the yeast mixture in this. Warm in a saucepan the rest of the milk, the sugar, the eggs, the mahlepi, half the mastic and the 250 grms of butter; combine well. Put half this mixture in the bowl with the flour and yeast. Knead well. Melt the rest of the butter and keep it aside. Add the rest of the mixture (eggs, milk, sugar, mahlepi, the mastic and the butter) to the flour and yeast mixture. Continue kneading, greasing your hands with the melted butter which you have beside you. The dough should be of a good consistency, neither stiff nor runny. More flour may be needed. Place the dough, covered with a clean cloth, in a warm place to rise. When it has risen enough, it is ready. Separate the dough into 3 thick strips and plait them. Paint it with beaten egg and sprinkle with the almonds and the rest of the mastic. Decorate the plait with a red hard boiled egg at one end. Bake in a moderate heated oven for 45 minutes approximately.

Christmas and New Year

There are plenty of traditions in Greece about Christmas, too. The house will be prepared, the tree put in place and a riot of baking will produce the special Christmas sweets. The table will groan under a variety of whatever the earth can produce in the depths of winter: fruit, almonds, walnuts, dried figs, raisins, and much, much more.

Today, of course, the sweets are more likely to come from a patisserie; the pastry-cooks work overtime at Christmas to keep up with demand. The turkey, too, has made its appearance on the Greek Christmas table, ousting the sucking pig which was traditionally bred and raised by the household specifically to be roasted and eaten on Christmas Day. Turkey may be the main dish, but there will be plenty of typically Greek mezedes to begin with and sweets and other delicacies to round off the meal.

New Year's Eve sees the house ready for celebration. The carefully-laid table has the 'vasilopita', the special New Year cake, at its centre. Somewhere the cake conceals a coin, and when it is cut among good-humoured wishes for the coming year, whoever finds the coin in his piece is assured of 365 days' good luck.

christmas soup
(soúpa christouyeniátiki)

1 portion, calories: 400.
Cooking time: 2 hours, 20 mins.

portions: 8-10

250   *grms of turkey*
250   *grms of beef*
250   *grms of lamb*
250   *grms of pork*
1 ½ *cups of rice*
3   *eggs*
3   *lemons, salt, pepper*

Boil all the meat and remove the scum that forms just before boiling point, then salt the meat. Lower the heat and allow to simmer for approximately 2 hours in plenty of water. Strain the stock. Bring it to the boil again and then add the rice. When the rice has cooked, prepare the egg and lemon sauce. Beat the eggs, adding the lemon juice drop by drop. Take in a ladle some of the stock and add it slowly to the egg and lemon mixture, stirring constantly. Finally, empty the egg and lemon mixture into the soup, which has been removed from the heat. Serve with freshly milled pepper.

stuffed turkey
(galopoúla yemistí)

1 portion (turkey, stuffing and a few potatoes), calories: 790.
Cooking time: 3 hours.

portions: 12-14

1   *turkey, 3 kilos*
300 *grms of mince*
1/2 *cup of rice*
1/3 *cup of pine nuts*
1   *onion, finely chopped*
1   *cup of white wine*
1 ½ *cups of butter*
3   *lemons*
      salt
      pepper
2   *kilos potatoes*

Clean the turkey and wash it well. Rub it all over —inside and out— with lemon juice. Prepare the stuffing. Put the onion with the mince into a frying pan and allow to cook till all its own juice has been absorbed. Then add half the butter to brown the mince. Add salt and pepper, the pine nuts and the rice. Stir for a while, then add the wine. Once this has been absorbed, add half a cup of water and allow this mixture to cook for a while. Stuff the turkey with the mixture through the stomach cavity and the hollow part of the neck. Then sew up these openings with needle and thread. Spread the bird with butter after salting it and peppering it. Wash and cut the potatoes into slices. Salt and pepper them and array them around the bird in the baking tin. Put in the rest of the butter and the juice of the lemons. Add 2 cups of water and roast for 3 hours very slowly.

roast sucking pig
(gourounópoulo sti soúvla)

1 portion, calories: 390.
Cooking time: 3 hours.

1	*small piglet*
	salt, pepper
1	*cup of oil*
2	*lemons*

Remove all bristles from the piglet and wash it well. Pass the spit through the pig, holding it by its backbone, which should be parallel with the spit. Rub the pig all over inside and out with lemon juice. Salt and pepper it well. Tie the legs to the spit and sew up the stomach cavity (all the innards will previously have been removed) with needle and thread. Allow the spitted pig to stand for 1-2 hours to dry out. Light a charcoal fire and once it has burnt down, put the spit into position and spit roast the pig, turning it very frequently so that it cooks evenly on all sides. From time to time, give it a good sprinkling of oil and lemon juice to make the skin crisp.

sugared almond cakes
(kourabiédes)

1 sugared almond cake, calories: 115.
Cooking time: 30-35 minutes.

1	kilo of flour (or 1 kilo and 280 grms)
640	grms of good butter
1/4	kilo of blanched, roasted almonds, crushed
2	egg yolks
150	grms of sugar
2	small spoonfuls of baking powder
3/4	cup of water
	a little rosewater
5	soupspoonfuls of brandy
1/2	kilo of caster sugar, or icing sugar

Beat the butter until it whitens, then add the egg yolks and sugar, the water, the almonds, the flour and the baking powder. It depends on the quality of the flour whether more than a kilo is needed. The dough should be stiff but easy to knead. Shape the cakes into rounds or half moons. Place them spaced evenly on an ungreased baking tray. Bake them for about 30-35 minutes.

As soon as you remove them hot from the oven, put them on to a bigger baking tray, sprinkle them with the rosewater and then sprinkle them very generously with the caster or icing sugar, making sure that the sugar covers each cake fully.

Once they have cooled, place them on a flat dish.

honey cakes
(melomakárona)

1 honey cake, calories: 95.
Cooking time: 30-35 minutes.

1	cup of good quality butter
1	cup of light olive oil
1	kilo of self-raising flour
1	cup of sugar
1	small spoonful of cinnamon
1/2	small spoonful of ground cloves
	grated peel from 2 oranges
1	small spoonful of baking soda
1	cup of strained yoghurt
1	cup of walnuts, chopped

for the syrup:

2	glasses of sugar
3	glasses of water
3	glasses of honey
	juice of 1 lemon
	walnuts and cinnamon for sprinkling

Put the self-raising flour and the butter into a large mixing bowl. Beat the butter well, adding the oil, then add the sugar, the cinnamon, the cloves, the grated orange peel, the soda and the yoghurt. Knead well and add the walnuts to the dough. Then divide the dough into portions and roll into small cigar shapes; bake them in the oven till browned. Ensure that when they are put into the baking tin, they are not too close to one another or too big, because they will swell. When they have cooled, prepare the syrup. Put the sugar with the water to boil for 10 minutes, then add the honey. Coat the cakes with the syrup in the following way. As the syrup is boiling, put as many of the little cakes into the pan as will fit comfortably. Allow to boil for 1 minute; remove immediately and place on a baking tray. When all the cakes have been treated in the syrup, supplement the boiling syrup with 1-2 cups of water. Once it has boiled again, put 3-4 cakes at a time in a straining spoon and dip them back in the syrup for 1 minute again. Then sprinkle with the walnuts and cinnamon. Treat the rest of the cakes in the same way.

christmas bread
(vasilópita)

1 portion, calories: 260.
Cooking time: 60 minutes.

500	grms of butter
500	grms of sugar
500	grms of warm milk
15	grms of crushed mastic
1 1/2	kilos of flour
	aniseed flavouring
5	eggs
50	grms of yeast
	a little salt
1	egg for glazing,
	sesame seeds

Put the flour in a bowl and make a 'well' in it; put in the eggs, the butter, the sugar, the milk and the crushed mastic, the aniseed, the salt and the yeast. Bind all the ingredients well into a dough. If the dough is stiff, warm milk can be used to make it more manageable. Cover the bowl with a clean cloth and allow to stand in a warm place for the dough to rise. When it has risen suffiently, knead it again and spread it in a buttered baking tin. Paint it with the beaten egg and sprinkle with sesame seeds.

Bake in a very hot oven to begin with, until the bread begins to brown, then lower heat to moderate and bake for about an hour.

Every place we visit leaves its set of memories engraved upon our minds. Those memories will be of sounds, colours, scents and —not the least important— tastes. The taste of some particular dish may remind us of a place not just because we happened to eat it there but, in the case of some kinds of food, because it is difficult to come across elsewhere. Some of the local specialities of Greece have become so popular that they are now cooked everywhere and are to be found on the menus of the best restaurants.

That is why we have collected the local recipes which you will find on the pages which follow and which you may already have encountered 'in the field'. And if reading these recipes brings to mind some happy holiday, imagine what tasting the food again will do for you.

lamb pasties (Mainland Greece)
(arní exochikó)

1 portion, calories: 710.
Cooking time: 60 minutes.

portions: 5

1	kilo of leg of lamb
1	cup of butter
10	small potatoes
5	whole onions
5	cloves of garlic
1/2	cup of grated kefalotiri cheese
5	pieces of feta cheese
5	sheets of ready-made fyllo pastry
	salt, pepper, rigani, oil

Cut the lamb into 5 portions and put it into a small pan with some butter, the potatoes and the onions to brown slightly. Separate each sheet of pastry, coat with butter and put 1 portion of meat, 1 whole peeled clove of garlic, 2 small potatoes, 1 small onion, 1 piece of kefalotiri and a little rigani on each. Add some more butter and fold the pastry into a pasty.

Coat the roasting tin with oil; coat the pasties with butter, cover them with aluminium foil and leave them to cook in a moderate oven for about 1 hour.

fried courgette flowers (Andros)
(kolokitholoúlouda tiganitá)

1 portion, calories: 280.
Cooking time: 15-20 minutes.

portions: 6

	the flowers of 12 courgettes
3	eggs
5	tablespoonfuls of flour
1/2	cup of grated cheese
3	tablespoonfuls of water
	oil for frying, salt

Clean and wash the flowers well. Then chop them up finely. Beat the eggs and mix them with the courgette flowers, the cheese and the flour. Salt and add the water. Heat the oil and fry the mixture by taking 1 big tablespoonful and dropping it into the hot oil. When the pancakes have browned on one side, flip them over and brown the other.

patatou (Tinos)
(patatoú)

1 portion, calories: 320.
Cooking time: 60 minutes.

portions: 8-10

1	kilo of potatoes
4	beaten eggs
1	cup of grated cheese (kefalotiri)
1/2	cup of crushed rusk
1	small bunch of parsley, finely chopped
1	tablespoonful of butter
	nutmeg, salt, pepper

Peel and wash the potatoes. Boil them and mash with a potato masher. Put them in a large bowl and mix with the cheese, the eggs, the crushed rusk and the finely chopped parsley. Combine well and add the nutmeg, the salt and the pepper.

Use half of the butter to coat the roasting tin. Spread the mixture, which should be quite thick, evenly. Take a fork and make a pattern on the surface. Sprinkle with the rest of the butter. Roast in a moderate oven for 1 hour. To be served hot, cut in squares or diamond shaped pieces.

stuffed kid or lamb (Naxos)
(katsikáki i arní patoúdo)

1 portion, calories: 440.
(With stuffing), calories: 780
Cooking time: 3 hours.

1	small kid or lamb, not exceeding, 6 kilos, with offal
1	kilo of spring onions, finely sliced
1	small bunch of dill, finely chopped
1/2	kilo of kefalotiri cheese (from Naxos, if at all possible)
1/4	kilo of bacon or salted pork fat
1 1/2	cups of rice
2	cups of good quality butter
	salt, pepper

Clean the lamb or kid and wash it well. Dice the offal and slice the onions. Put in a large frying pan or saucepan 1 cup of butter, the offal and the onions and cook lightly. Add the bacon, the rice, the dill, the salt and the pepper and a minimum amount of water and allow to cook altogether for about 2-3 minutes. This is the stuffing. Now remove it from the heat, cut the cheese into pieces and add it to the mixture. Stuff the lamb or kid with it and sew up the cavity using a large needle and strong thread. Salt and pepper it and then coat it with the rest of the butter. If you wish to roast it in an electric oven, tie it in a circle so that the hind and front legs touch. Roast in a moderate oven for 3 hours.

roast snails (Paros)
(salingária psitá)

1 portion, calories: 160.
Cooking time: 15 minutes.

portions: 6-8

1	kilo of snails
	salt, rigani, vinegar, oil, lemon

Put the snails in water overnight, covering them with a heavy lid to prevent their escape. The ones that come out of their shells are alive and are suitable for cooking. Wash them thoroughly to remove all slimy substances produced in the shells and sprinkle with vinegar. Grill them over charcoal with the opening of the shells downwards for a quarter of an hour. Then remove them from their shells and serve with lemon and oil and sprinkled with rigani.

onion pie (Mykonos)
(kremmidópita)

1 portion, calories: 300.
Cooking time: 20-30 minutes.

1	kilo of soft, fresh, unsalted white cheese
1/2	cup of butter
3	eggs, 3 spring onions
1	small bundle of white beets, a little dill
8	sheets of fyllo pastry

Chop the onions and the beets finely. Salt and twist the beets to remove as much excess water as possible. Add the white cheese, the dill (finely chopped beforehand), adding salt to this too and combine these ingredients. Spread half of the sheets of pastry in a medium sized baking tin, buttering each sheet before spreading, then add the onion mixture to tin. Spread mixture evenly and then spread the rest of the sheets on top, not forgetting to butter each one as before. Once the filling is covered, take a sharp knife and divide the surface of the pie into equal portions to facilitate serving when pie is done. Sprinkle with water and cook in moderate oven for about 20-30 minutes.

tomato balls (Santorini)
(pseftokeftédes)

1 portion, calories: 200.
Cooking time: 10 minutes.

portions: 8

500	grms of ripe tomatoes
2	large onions, finely chopped
2	small bunches of mint, finely chopped
	salt, pepper and cinnamon
	flour
	oil for frying

Skin and chop up the tomatoes. Add to them salt and pepper and the mint, the onion and the cinnamon and knead together in a large bowl. Add as much flour as is needed to obtain a very soft paste. Put oil in a frying pan and heat well. Then take a large tablespoon and spoon in the mixture into the hot oil. When the tomato balls are browned on one side, turn them over to brown evenly on the other. Serve hot.

pan bread (Santorini)
(tiganópsoma)

1 portion, calories: 230.
Cooking time: 8 minutes.

portions: 8-9

2	cups of flour
2-3	spring onions, finely chopped
2	ripe tomatoes, skinned and crushed
1	cup of water
	salt, pepper, oil for frying

Mix the flour with the water and add the crushed tomatoes, the onion and the salt and pepper. Combine the mixture well with a wooden spoon to form a smooth cream. Put oil into a frying pan and heat it well. Fry the pan bread by spooning it with a large tablespoon into the hot oil. When one side has browned, turn it to brown evenly on the other.

snail stew (Crete)
(salingária stifádo)

1 portion, calories: 290.
Cooking time: 30-40 minutes.

portions: 4-6

1	*kilo of large snails*
1	*kilo of spring onions*
1 ½	*cups of oil*
7	*cloves of garlic*
1/2	*cup of vinegar*
1	*teaspoonful of rosemary*
3	*bay leaves*
5	*ripe tomatoes*
	salt
	pepper

Put the snails in a pot with water to stand overnight. Cover with something heavy so that they don't escape. Wash them well, removing all dirt.

Put them on to heat with water. When some scum begins to appear on the surface, usually just before boiling, add salt and stir vigorously, always in the same direction. Boil for about 15 minutes. Take a knife —this should be very sharp— and make a hole in the back of the shell. Rinse them well in water in which they have been boiled so that they don't lose their taste.

Skin and wash the onions. Put the oil, the onions and the garlic in a saucepan to brown. Add the tomatoes, skinned and chopped, the bay leaves, the rosemary and the salt and pepper. Supplement with water, then cover and allow to simmer. When the onions are almost ready, add the snails and allow to simmer together until moisture has been absorbed and only sauce remains. It is ready to serve.

Snail stew is a marvellous appetizer, which you will find in many Greek tavernas. If the snails are collected from an area where there is a lot thyme, they will be even tastier.

kalitsounia (Crete)
with savoury mezithra

1 portion, calories: 140.
Cooking time: 30 minutes.

for the pastry:

1	cup of oil
1	glass of water
	the juice of 1 lemon
	a little salt
1	kilo of flour (or as much as is needed)

for the filling:

1 1/2	kilos of savoury mezithra cheese
3	eggs
	mint
	sesame seeds
1	egg for glazing

Mix the oil with the lemon juice, adding salt. Add the flour little by little until you form a dough which is manageable. Roll out the dough into a sheet of average thickness. Cut it into rounds with the aid of the rim of a glass. Prepare the filling by combining well the mezithra, the eggs, the mint and a little salt. Fill each round of dough with this mixture with the help of a teaspoon and fold over the pieces of dough into half moon shapes. Pinch the edges of the pastry with the fingers to close well. Coat with the egg and sprinkle the sesame seeds. Bake in a moderate oven for 30 minutes.

kalitsounia (Crete)
with sweet mezithra

1 portion, calories: 220.
Cooking time: 30 minutes.

600	grms of sugar
1/2	cup of oil, 1/2 cup of butter
1	cup of milk, 6 eggs
1	teaspoonful of baking powder
1	teaspoonful of baking soda
2	sticks of vanilla
2	kilos of flour (or as much as is needed)

for the filling:

1 1/2	kilos of unsalted mezithra or anthotiro cheese; cinnamon, mint
1	cup of sugar; 1 egg (for glazing)

Beat together the butter, oil and sugar. Add the eggs one by one and the vanilla. Combine the baking powder with the flour and dissolve the soda in the milk. Use as much of the 2 kilos of flour as is necessary to make a dough which can be handled. Roll it out thick and cut into squares of 10 x 10 centimetres. Prepare the filling by combining the sugar, the mezithra, the cinnamon and the mint. With a soupspoon as a measure, spoon this mixture on to each square of pastry. Fold two corners towards the centre, then fold the other two over to the edges of these, maintaining a square shape. Coat with the egg and sprinkle with cinnamon; bake for 30 minutes in a moderate oven.

Aegean sea-food (Hydra)
(thalassiná tou egéou)

1 portion, calories: 550.
Cooking time: 40-50 minutes.

portions: 10

250	grms of shrimps
500	grms of mussels
250	grms of squid
1	cuttlefish
1	small octopus
1 ½	cups of oil
1	onion, grated
2	cups of rice
	salt, pepper

Clean and wash the sea food well. Boil each species separately and keep the shrimp and mussel juice only. Chop up all the sea food.

Put into a large frying pan the cup of oil, the onion and the sea food. Fry lightly. In a saucepan put the other half cup of oil, add the rice and heat till transparent.

Then douse it with the juice of the shrimps and mussels.

Add the mixture of sea food and 3 cups of hot water and allow to boil till only the oil remains.

stuffed sea urchins
(Spetses)
(achiní yemistí)

1 portion, calories: 350.
Cooking time: 40-45 minutes.

portions: 7

14   sea urchins, cleaned and free from
     sand
1 ½ cups of rice
1   medium-sized onion, finely chopped
1   cup of oil
3   ripe tomatoes
     salt, pepper

Remove the spines of the sea urchins with the help of a sharp knife and also by rubbing any that remain on a clean stone. Wash them carefully without dipping them in water. Open them carefully on the side where the little teeth are situated. Allow the sea water to drip into a bowl and keep this aside. Remove the sand and detach the eggs from the sides of the interior but do not take them out. Put the oil with the onion in a saucepan to brown. Add the parsley, the salt, the pepper and the tomatoes, which should have been skinned and finely chopped, then finally the rice. Allow to boil together for a while. Stuff all the sea urchins one by one with this mixture, taking care to leave enough room for the swelling of the rice. Then arrange them in a wide, flat pan. Strain the sea water that you have kept back to remove any unwanted particles. Add this to the stuffing. Put some more oil and water in the pan. Cover the stuffed urchins with a plate and allow to simmer for half an hour.

filiani dolmades (Lesvos)

1 portion, calories: 340.
Cooking time: 30-40 minutes.

portions: 8-10

6   very large onions
300 grms of minced veal
300 grms of minced pork
1   medium-sized onion, finely chopped
1/2 cup of rice
1 ½ cups of oil
     salt
     pepper
     cinnamon

Skin the onions, nick them vertically on one side and scald them in hot water for ten minutes. Knead the minced meats with the rice, the finely chopped onion and the salt and pepper.

Separate off the largest of the outer onion layers and put on each one 2 teaspoonfuls of the mixture and roll it up.

Place them in a saucepan in circles, one circle on top of the other. Add the oil and then cover with a heavy plate to prevent them from opening during the cooking process. Allow to boil on a medium heat for 30-40 minutes so that they absorb the moisture and leave only the oil.

To be served cold in a flat dish, sprinkled with cinnamon.

This is a special dish from Lesvos for Christmas and the New Year.

'feast' (Samos)
(yiortí)

1 portion, calories: 700.
Cooking time: 50-60 minutes.

portions: 8

1/2   kilo of pork
1/2   kilo of goat meat
5   onions, finely chopped
1/2   kilo of wheat
1   cup of oil
1/2   cup of butter
      salt, pepper, cinnamon

Grind the corn so that the grains are cut into 2 or three pieces. Cut the meat into small portions and put it into a saucepan with water. Heat and skim off the scum that appears on the surface. Put in a generous amount of salt and add the onions and the oil. Allow to boil for 30-40 minutes and supplement with water. Add the corn, stirring constantly to avoid sticking. When it is ready, heat the butter very well and pour it over the ingredients of the saucepan. To be served sprinkled with pepper and cinnamon.

pasta with yoghurt (Kos)
(zimarikó me yiaoúrti)

1 portion, calories: 570.

portions: 4-6

1/2   kilo of pasta (spirals or short macaroni)
1   kilo of strained yoghurt
3   large onions, finely chopped
1/2   cup of butter, salt

Boil the pasta in salted water and drain. Put the yoghurt in a large bowl; add the hot pasta and combine. Put the onion with the butter in a frying pan to brown. Spread half the quantity of macaroni in a large, flat dish and spread half of the onion on it. Cover this layer with more macaroni and the rest of the onion on top of this.

cabbage with mince
(Chios)
(láhano me kimá)

1 portion, calories: 395.
Cooking time: 40 minutes.

portions: 4-6

1   kilo of cabbage
600   grms of mince
1 1/2 cups of oil
1   onion, finely chopped, salt, pepper
3   tomatoes, skinned and crushed
      half a tablespoonful of fresh butter

Cut the cabbage into large chunks and wash well. Boil the chunks for a short while and drain. Put oil with the finely chopped onion on to heat, add the mince. Allow its moisture to be absorbed, then add the tomatoes, the cabbage chunks and salt and pepper. Supplement with enough water and allow to simmer till only the oil remains. When the cabbage is tender, add the fresh butter and stir.

spicy whitebait (Rhodes)
(marída pikántiki)

1 portion, calories: 280.

portions: 4

1/2   kilo of whitebait
1   onion, finely chopped
1   ripe tomato
      parsley and mint, both finely chopped
3   tablespoonfuls of flour
1   egg, beaten, oil, salt and pepper

Wash the fish and remove heads and tails. In a large bowl, combine the onion, the parsley, the mint, the tomato (skinned and as finely chopped as possible), the flour, the egg, and salt and pepper. Add the whitebait to this and combine well. Put oil in a frying pan and put on to heat. When it is well heated, fry the mixture by spooning it into the oil with a large tablespoon. To be served with green salad or village salad.

noodles (Rhodes)
(hilopítes)

1 portion, calories: 450.

to make the noodles:

2	kilos of flour
6	eggs, as much milk as needed

to cook the noodles:

2	cups of noodles
1/2	kilo of ripe tomatoes, skinned
1	tablespoonful of butter, salt

To make the noodles: In a large bowl prepare a dough with the flour, the eggs and as much milk as needed to make a dough to be rolled out in sheets. Roll out the sheets of dough one by one, then cut them into narrow strips. Then cut the strips into squares and lay them out to dry.

To cook the noodles: Put into a saucepan the butter, the skinned tomatoes and enough water. When this boils, add the noodles and allow to simmer, stirring constantly to avoid sticking. Simmer till all moisture has been absorbed.

bourdheto (Corfu)

1 portion, calories: 320.
Cooking time: 30-40 minutes.

portions: 6

1	kilo of rock fish
1/2	kilo of onions, finely chopped
1/2	kilo of ripe tomatoes
1	cup of oil
2	teaspoonfuls of red pepper
	salt
	pepper

Clean and wash the fish well. Salt and allow to stand. Put the onion in a pan to brown. Add the tomatoes, skinned and cut into small sections.

Also add the salt and the pepper and allow to simmer with a little water until a thick sauce is formed.

Spread the fish in layers in a saucepan, pouring the sauce over them. Add a little more water and allow to simmer for 30-40 minutes.

macaroni à la Corfu
(pastitsáda)

1 portion, calories: 700.
Cooking time: 90 minutes.

portions: 4-5

1	kilo of beef
1 1/2	cups of tomato juice
1/2	cup of red wine
4	onions, finely chopped
4-5	cloves of garlic
2	tablespoonfuls of butter
1/2	kilo of macaroni
	kefalotiri (hard Greek cheese)
	salt, pepper

Wash the meat well and with a sharp, pointed knife nick in several places and plug each hole with one clove of garlic. Sprinkle over it salt and pepper and put it in a saucepan with the butter and the finely chopped onion to brown. Douse with the wine and add the tomato juice. Add water and allow to simmer. When the meat is tender, boil the macaroni with plenty of salted water. To be served mixed with the grated cheese and the gravy of the meat. Serve one portion of meat with each plate.

sofrito (Corfu)

1 portion, calories: 670.
Cooking time: 60 minutes.

portions: 6-8

1	kilo of boneless veal or tender beef
1	kilo of potatoes
1/3	cup of oil
1/2	cup of vinegar
10	cloves of garlic, chopped
1	small bunch of parsley
	oil for frying
	flour, salt, pepper

Cut the meat into slices and pound the slices to flatten and tenderize it. Coat with

steak rolls (Zante)
(skaltsotséta)

1 portion, calories: 440.
Cooking time: 60 minutes.

portions: 8

1	kilo of steak
2	large cloves of garlic, finely chopped
1	small bunch of parsley, finely chopped
250	grms of feta cheese
1	kilo of ripe tomatoes
1/2	cup kefalotiri or other hard cheese, grated
1/3	cup of crushed rusk
1/2	cup of oil, salt, pepper

Make a mixture with the garlic, the parsley, the rusk, the cheeses and 2 of the tomatoes, which have been skinned and crushed beforehand. Combine the ingredients with salt and pepper.

Cut the meat into fine slices with a sharp knife. Put on each slice a small portion of the mixture, roll it up and fasten with a toothpick. Put oil in a pan and heat it. When the oil is well heated, brown the steak rolls in it. Skin the rest of the tomatoes and add them to the pan, adding water. Simmer the steak rolls until tender.

flour and fry the slices in oil on a high heat. Peel the potatoes and cut them into round slices and fry these too. In a large bowl combine the chopped garlic, the parsley, finely chopped, the salt and the pepper. Take a wide, flat pan, spread one layer of potato and sprinkle with a portion of the mixture. Then spread over this, a layer of meat and sprinkle this too with the mixture from the bowl and continue in this way until all the ingredients are used up. Finally, pour over the oil and the vinegar and allow to simmer for about 1 hour.

spetsofáï (Pelion)

1 portion, calories: 350.
Cooking time: 40 minutes.

portions: 6-8

1	kilo of small, slim, green peppers
4	village sausages, from Pelion if possible, otherwise a very spicy variety
1	kilo of ripe tomatoes
2	onions, finely chopped
1 ½	cups of oil
	salt, pepper, a little sugar

Wash and drain the peppers. Fry them in 1 cup of oil to brown well. Remove them from the frying pan and fry the sausages, which have been finely sliced.

After having fried them well, remove from pan and add to the pan the rest of the oil. Then add the tomatoes, having skinned and crushed them beforehand, the onions, very little salt and even less sugar. Allow this sauce to simmer for about 20 minutes. Add the peppers and the sausage and continue to simmer for a while longer till a thick sauce has formed.

Variation:
The sausages may be cooked whole, if preferred, and in this way will be more tender.

'Trachanas'

One traditional food with plenty of nourishing elements is 'trachanas'. There are a great many varieties of recipes from all over Greece. We have chosen for you recipes representing the good old days and it won't be difficult for you to try them. They will fully compensate for the time you dedicate to them.

savoury trachanas
(trachanás xinós)

1 ½	kilos ripe tomatoes
2	kilos of plain yoghurt
1/2	kilo of onions
3	kilos of thick semolina
3	tablespoonfuls of salt

Skin the tomatoes, removing the seeds, and mash them. Skin, then finely chop the onions. Put the onions and tomatoes with the salt into a small saucepan to boil well until a thick sauce is formed. Allow this sauce to cool, then pour it into a bowl and combine with the yoghurt. Add the semolina to the mixture. More semolina may be required. The paste should be of a thick consistency but not stick to the hands. Spread a very clean tablecloth on a table in a shady part of the room (away from sunlight, that is). Take a small portion of the mixture, mould it into a small pat; there is no need to worry about the shape, but it should not be any bigger than the top of a drinking glass. Then place the pat on the tablecloth. Continue in this way with the rest of the mixture until it is used up. Allow the pats of trachanas to dry externally only, not thoroughly, and until the colour changes slightly. Take the trachanas and rub it through a sieve with wide mesh. The sieve should be placed up-side-down so that the rubbed trachanas falls on to the tablecloth. When it has been all been rubbed through, spread it evenly on the cloth to stand to dry for 10 days, occasionally turning it to dry on all sides. Finally, preserve in a clean cloth bag or a glass jar.

sweet trachanas
(trachanás glikós)

Cooking time: 30 minutes.

2	litres of full-cream milk
2	teaspoonfuls of salt
1	kilo of wheat, coarsely crushed

Put the milk to heat and as it starts to boil add the crushed corn gradually, stirring constantly with a wooden spoon so that it doesn't stick. Once it has thickened, remove from heat and allow to cool. Once cooled, divide into portions and spread out on a clean tablecloth and allow to dry out of sunlight. As soon as it has dried, rub through a sieve (with wide mesh) and allow to stand for 4 days to completely dry out. Keep in a glass jar or a clean cloth bag.

Cooking of savoury and sweet trachanas

1 dish of trachanas, calories: 330.
Cooking time: 20 minutes.

portions: 3-4

1/2	cup of trachanas
1	tablespoonful of butter
4	cups of water

Put the water with the butter on to heat. When it begins to boil, add the trachanas. Stir and allow to boil for a further 20 minutes. Add a little salt in the case of the savoury trachanas and serve hot.

Sweets

People with a sweet tooth —and there plenty of them— make sure that wherever they go they try the local sweets. That has led to some degree of internationalisation of the most tempting examples of the pastry-cook's art. There are some lucky people who can afford to travel to the country in which their favourite sweets are commonly made, but baking is an art which can be learned and is within the scope of all us, and so those without the means to travel can reproduce their favourite tastes without stirring from the kitchen. The recipes in this chapter will help you to do that.

Try one of these recipes whenever you want to give yourself —or someone else— a treat. They are all traditionally Greek. Or make a Greek 'spoon sweet' (preserve), another institution in the Greek household. These preserves are pure, containing only fruit and sugar, and they keep for many months. It is the tradition in Greece to serve them with a cup of Greek coffee and a tall glass of ice-cold water.

black cherry conserve
(víssino glikó)

1 teaspoon of conserve, calories: 100.
1 glass of sour cherry drink (that is, conserve diluted with water), calories: 150

1	kilo of black cherries
1	kilo + 200 grms of sugar
1	cup of water
1	teaspoonful of lemon juice

Spread in a saucepan one layer of cherries and cover them with sugar. Continue in this way: a layer of cherries, then cover with sugar. Then allow to stand for hours, then add water and bring to the boil on a high heat. When scum starts to form, remove with a skimmer and when the juice thickens, add the lemon juice, just before taking it off the heat. If you wish to make a drink of this black cherry syrup, add half a kilo more sugar to increase the syrup.

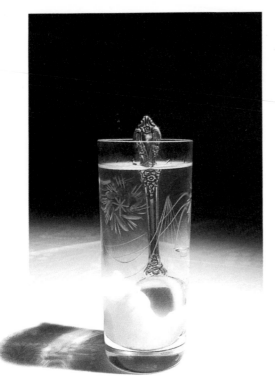

vanilla submarine
(vanília glikó - ipouríchio)

1 teaspoonful, calories: 80.

640	grms of sugar
1/2	cup of water
2	teaspoonfuls of lemon juice
1	level teaspoon of vanilla paste

Put the water to boil with the sugar and stir to begin with. When the syrup has thickened (this can be tested by dropping a tiny spot on a plate and seeing it doesn't melt), add the lemon juice and continue to boil for a while, then remove from heat. Pour it into an earthernware or enamel bowl and leave it cool to lukewarm. Then add the vanilla and stir with a wooden spoon and continue stirring in the same direction until it thickens. To be served on a teaspoon in a glass of water.

red cherry conserve
(kerási glikó)

1 teaspoon, calories: 100.

1	*kilo of red cherries*
1	*kilo of sugar*
1	*cup of water, vanilla*
1	*teaspoonful of lemon juice*

Choose large, hard cherries. Wash them well and remove the stems and leaves; also remove the stones with a special soop. Put the sugar and water on to boil, stirring at the start. As it starts to thicken, remove from heat and allow to cool a little. Then, add the cherries and put back on to heat, but this time at a high heat. Remove the scum that forms on the surface and once the syrup thickens again, add the lemon juice and vanilla. When it cools completely, keep in glass jars.

Variation: Sweet orange conserve can also be made with the peel of orange only. In this case, you don't need to cut the orange into sections; instead, you roll up the peel and tile with string and boil like this. You remove the string once the peel has thickened with boiling.

orange conserve
(portokáli glikó)

1 section of orange, calories: 110.
Cooking time: 60 minutes.

6	*large oranges with thick peel*
1 ½	*kilos of sugar*
3	*cups of water*
1	*teaspoon of lemon juice, vanilla*

Grate the rind of the oranges with the fine side of a grater and wash well. Boil the oranges whole. They are ready when you jab them with a toothpick and it doesn't stick. Drain them and cut each one vertically into four, then cut each orange again so that you get eight sections. Remove the white pith with scissors and take out any hard parts; allow to strain. Boil the sugar with the water and when it thickens, add the oranges. Continue boiling till the juice has thickened well. Add the lemon juice and the vanilla shortly before removing from heat.

halva (made with semolina)
(halvás me simigdáli)

1 portion, calories: 280.
Preparation time: 30 minutes.

1   *cup of oil*
1   *cup of fine semolina*
1   *cup of coarse semolina*
3   *cups of sugar*
4   *cups of water*
     cinnamon

Put oil in a saucepan to heat. Add the semolina and stir constantly allowing it to brown slightly. In the meantime, put the sugar with the water in another saucepan to boil for 10 minutes. When the semolina has browned, pour in the sugar syrup. Sprinkle liberally with the cinnamon and lower the heat; continue stirring until the mixture thickens.

The halva is ready when it is easily detached from the saucepan.

Place the halva in a mould and when it has cooled, remove from mould to a flat dish, sprinkling again with cinnamon.

Variation: If desired, almonds or pine nuts, browned at the beginning, may be added.

Ryna's halva
(halvás tis Rínas)

1 piece, calories: 430.
Cooking time: 40-50 minutes.

1	kilo of fine semolina
1/2	kilo of almonds, finely chopped
2	kilos of sugar
3	tablespoonfuls of cinnamon
1/2	kilo of butter
12	eggs, well beaten

Beat the butter well to whiten, add 1 kilo of sugar, the beaten eggs, the almonds, the cinnamon and finally the semolina. Coat a large baking tin (for an electric oven) with butter and pour the mixture in. Allow to bake for 40-50 minutes at 220°-240° covered with aluminium foil. When the surface browns, it is ready, but only cut when it has cooled.

Prepare the syrup with the other kilo of sugar and 3 glasses of water. A short time is required for boiling into a thin syrup solution.

rice pudding
(rizógalo)

1 portion, calories: 300.
Cooking time: 20 minutes.

1	litre of milk
1/2	cup of pudding rice
1	cup of water
4	tablespoonfuls of cornflour
	vanilla
2	tablespoonfuls of sugar
	cinnamon

Put the rice in water to boil. When the water has been absorbed, add the milk (keeping aside a cup to be used for the dissolving of the cornflour) and the sugar. Stir this constantly. When it starts to thicken, add the half cup of milk with the dissolved cornflour to it and continue stirring until the cream thickens.

To be served in small bowls or plates, sprinkled liberally with cinnamon.

moustalevria

1 portion, calories: 500.

7	*glasses of wine must already prepared*
1	*glass of fine semolina*
	crushed walnuts and almonds
	cinnamon

Use ready-prepared boiled must. (If the wine residue is not prepared, you will need, for a small amount of residue, 1 tablespoonful of wood ash. Yes, ash. Put it in a pan and boil with the ash, then strain it through a fine filter to clean. You will have to continue the boiling if it hasn't sweetened enough).

Put the 7 glasses of must in a saucepan to boil and add the semolina, stirring constantly with a wooden spoon.

When this starts to thicken, it is ready to be served in a little bowls or on plates, sprinkled liberally with the walnuts, almonds and cinnamon.

custard pie
(galatoboúreko)

1 portion, calories: 370.
Cooking time: 30 minutes.

12	ready-made sheets of fyllo pastry
1	cup of good quality butter
1/2	cup of sugar
4	glasses of milk
1	glass of fine semolina
6	eggs, beaten, vanilla

for the syrup:

4	glasses of sugar
2	glasses of water
	the peel of 1 lemon, vanilla
	the juice of half a lemon

Put in a saucepan the sugar and the milk to heat, adding the semolina a little at a time, stirring constantly. Before it thickens completely, remove from heat, wait until the boiling ceases then add the eggs and the vanilla very gradually. Spread the 6 sheets of pastry in an oblong baking tin, coating each one with butter, which should have been melted beforehand. Then spread the mixture in the tin evenly and cover with the other 6 sheets of pastry, coating each one as before. Mark out the top sheet into squares with a knife to make serving easier once the pastry has cooled. Allow the oven to heat and bake the sweet for about 30 minutes. Prepare the syrup: Put the 4 glasses of sugar and the water in a saucepan and boil for 10 minutes, adding the lemon peel, the lemon juice and the vanilla. Pour the syrup hot over the custard pie, then cut to serve once it has cooled.

baclavas

1 piece, calories: 590.
Cooking time: 60 minutes.

1	kilo of ready-made sheets of fyllo pastry
1	kilo of almonds, finely crushed
400	grms of buttermilk
2	tablespoonfuls of cinnamon
	whole cloves

for the syrup:

2	kilos of sugar
6	glasses of water
	vanilla
	the juice of 1 lemon

Mix the crushed almonds with the cinnamon. Melt the butter and coat a baking tin with it. Spread the sheets of pastry, coating each with butter. Begin with 3 sheets then sprinkle each sheet with crushed almonds and cinnamon and cover it with the next sheet. Divide the sprinkling ingredients so that 4 sheets will be left over without any sprinkling. Coat the last sheet of pastry with butter and mark out the baclavas with a knife into diamond shaped pieces. Plug each piece with 1 clove in its centre. Allow to bake in a moderate oven for 60-70 minutes. Prepare the syrup, but don't make it too thick. When the baclavas has cooled, pour the syrup over it.

kataïfi

1 piece, calories: 390.
Cooking time: 30-40 minutes.

1	kilo of ready-made kataïfi pastry
500	grms of almond kernels
1 ½	tablespoonfuls of cinnamon
2	tablespoonfuls of crushed rusk
2	cups of buttermilk

for the syrup:

1 ½	kilos of sugar
4	glasses of water
	the juice of 1 lemon
	vanilla

Pound the almonds and mix with the cinnamon and the crushed rusk. Coat a baking tin with butter. Take one piece of the pastry and spread it on it one tablespoonful of the mixture. Roll it up into a sausage roll shape and place in the baking tin. Continue in the same way with the rest of the pastry and when all of them are rolled up, put the butter on to heat. When it has melted sufficiently, pour it over (1 full tablespoonful) each roll. Allow the rolls to bake in a moderate oven for 40-50 minutes until lightly browned. Allow to cool, then prepare the syrup. Boil the sugar with the water, add the vanilla and the juice of the lemon and then pour it slowly over the rolls.

walnut cake
(karidópita)

1 piece, calories: 400.
Cooking time: 60 minutes.

1	cup of sugar
1	cup of milk
1/2	cup of butter
2	cups of roughly crushed walnuts
	cinnamon, ground cloves
1 ½	cups of crushed rusk
1 ½	cups of flour
5	eggs
1	teaspoonful of baking soda
3	teaspoonfuls of baking powder
2	tablespoonfuls of brandy

for the syrup:

3	cups of sugar
2	cups of water
1	tablespoonful of lemon juice

Beat the butter and add the sugar and the eggs. Pour the milk in and add the walnuts, which should have been mixed with the ground cloves and the cinnamon, the soda dissolved in the brandy, the crushed rusk and the flour mixed with the baking powder. Combine all this well and spread it in a baking tin coated with butter. Before spreading the mixture in the tin, sprinkle it lightly with flour.

Bake for about 1 hour in a hot oven to begin with, then reducing the heat after a while. Prepare the syrup and pour it over the walnut cake.

oil cake
(glikó tapsioú me ládi)

1 piece, calories: 350.
Cooking time: 40-50 minutes.

1 ½   glasses of oil
1 ½   glasses of orange juice
1 ½   cups of sugar
2-3   tablespoonfuls of brandy
1   teaspoonful of baking soda
1   teaspoonful of cinnamon
1   teaspoonful of ground cloves
1/2   cup of walnuts
1/2   cup of raisins
600   grms of flour
      a few sesame seeds, a little oil

Combine the oil, the orange juice and the sugar. Dissolve the soda with the brandy and add it to the mixture also; add the cinnamon and the ground cloves. Then very gradually add the flour, stirring constantly. Finally, combine the walnuts and the raisins with the mixture. Coat a medium-sized baking tin and pour the mixture into it. Shake the tin to spread the mixture evenly. Sprinkle with sesame seeds and bake for 40-50 minutes. Cut to serve into oblong pieces.

oil cookies
(koulourákia ladioú)

1 cooky, calories: 80.
Cooking time: 30 minutes.

1   glass of oil
1   glass of orange juice
1   glass of sugar
      the juice of one lemon
1   teaspoonful of baking soda
1   teaspoonful of baking powder
1   tablespoonful of grated orange rind
1   kilo of flour, or a little more may
      be needed

Combine the oil, the orange juice, the sugar and grated orange rind. Dissolve the soda in the lemon juice and add this solution to the mixture of the other ingredients. Mix the baking powder with the flour and add it to the mixture a little at a time.

Knead well until it becomes a thick dough.

Separate the dough into thin strips and plait plaits or mould into any shape desired. Bake in a moderate oven for 30 minutes.

turnovers
(díples)

1 turnover, calories: 90.

2 ½   cups of flour
3   eggs
4   tablespoonfuls of brandy
1   teaspoonful of baking powder
2   tablespoonfuls of sugar
       oil for frying
1   cup of honey
1/2   cup of warm water
       coarsely chopped walnuts
       cinnamon

Mix the flour with the baking powder in a bowl. Make a well in the centre. Beat the eggs with the sugar and the brandy and add this to the flour, kneading well. Allow the dough to stand for half an hour and knead again. (Maybe half a cup of flour more may be required, but do not add this until you are sure if it is needed). Roll out the dough into a thin sheet then cut it into strips which can be tied in bows or knots or any shape you wish. Put plenty of oil in a frying pan to heat.

The turnovers must be fried in very hot oil. When they have browned lightly, remove them from the heat and allow them to drain on absorbent kitchen paper.

Prepare the honey syrup by dissolving the honey in warm water. Pour it over the turnovers, which have been placed on a flat dish.

Sprinkle with walnuts and cinnamon.

honey puffs
(loukoumádes)

1 portion, calories: 290.

portions: 8-10

650   grms of flour
1   full tablespoonful of yeast
1   cup of lukewarm water
1   tablespoonful of salt
      oil for frying

for the syrup:

2   cups of sugar
1   cup of honey
1   cup of water
      cinnamon

Put the flour in a bowl and mix it with the salt. Make a well in the centre and put in the yeast, having melted it first in the lukewarm water. Combine the mixture, adding more lukewarm water to make a medium dough. Knead it for a little while then place the dough, covered with a clean cloth, in a warm place to rise. When it has done so (you can judge this by the small bubbles that will have formed on the surface), it is ready.

In a deep pan put plenty of oil to heat. Wet your hands and take a piece of the dough squeezing it in your fist to allow a small amount of the dough to be forced through the opening between your thumb and forefinger. Take a spoon and wet it,

bougatsa
(bougátsa)

1 piece, calories: 340.
Cooking time: 20 minutes.

6   sheets of ready-made fyllo pastry
3   cups of milk
5   tablespoonfuls of sugar
5   tablespoonfuls of semolina
2   eggs, beaten
3   tablespoonfuls of butter
1   cup of castor sugar
1/2   tablespoonful of cinnamon

Put in a small saucepan the sugar, the milk and the semolina to heat on a moderate flame. Stir till it has thickened slightly. Remove from heat and add the eggs gradually, stirring well. Spread 1 sheet of pastry with melted butter. Put in the centre of the pastry a small portion of the mixture, remembering to divide the mixture so that you have enough for 5 more sheets. Fold the pastry over the filling carefully to form a square shape. Repeat this procedure with the other 5 sheets. Coat the top sheet with butter. Grease the baking tin and bake in a moderate oven for about 20 minutes.

When cooked, sprinkle with castor sugar and cinnamon.

then scoop the dough from between your thumb and forefinger and place it in the boiling oil. When the puffs have browned slightly, remove from the oil and place on absorbent kitchen paper.

To be served on a flat dish with the syrup poured over them.

Prepare the syrup as follows: Boil the sugar with the water and the honey for 3-4 minutes. Once the honey puffs have been placed on the dish for serving and the syrup poured over, sprinkle with cinnamon.

Greek coffee

A dictionary of Greek coffee

coffee: Greek coffee is made from beans ground very fine indeed, to the consistency of a powder.

briki: the briki is the coffee-pot for Greek coffee. Brikia come in number of different sizes and all have long handles.

koupaki or flytsanaki (coffee-cups): Greek coffee is traditionally served in very small white china cups.

kaïmaki: this is the thick layer of froth which forms on top of the coffee as it nears the boil. It should not be disturbed when pouring the coffee.

katakathi (grounds): Greek coffee is served with the grounds, and so the whole cupful cannot be drunk. There will always be a thick sediment at the bottom.

In the traditional Greek coffee-shop the range of refreshments is limited: ouzo, with perhaps a sliver of octopus as a mezes, Turkish delight with a glass of cold water, preserves and, of course, Greek coffee. Greek coffee is very strong, and its powerful aroma permeates the coffee-shop. Coffe-drinking, an old eastern custom, passed via the Arabs to the Greeks of Constantinople and Asia Minor and was incorporated into their way of life. Although there are now many varieties of instant and percolated coffee on the market in Greece, there has been no reduction in the demand for the traditional way of doing things.

In days gone by, the daily recreation of men in Greek towns and villages was to go to the coffee-shop and, over a cup of Greek coffee, read the paper and talk politics with the other locals. Even today in the towns of Eastern Macedonia and Thrace one will come across old men for whom coffee-making is a complete ritual: first the coffee beans are slowly roasted, then they are ground fine in a hand-mill. Next, the coffee is made in the old brass briki, among the embers of the fire. The whole process can take up to half an hour, but the taste produced is unique and unforgettable.

Ordinary coffee-drinkers, of course, need not take all this trouble, since Greek coffee is sold ready-ground today. But those who relish coffee as it ought to be could do worst than buy the beans and grind them at home: it really does make a difference to the taste.

Recipes for Greek coffee follow. Time for a cup, then, and your good health!

'heavy' coffee
(kafés varýs glykós)

Preparation time: 10 minutes.

1   small cup of water
1½-2 teaspoonfuls of sugar
1   teaspoonful of coffee

Put the water into the 'briki' to heat. While it is getting hot, add the sugar and coffee. Stir. As soon as it rises, remove from heat before it boils completely so as not to spoil the froth.

medium coffee
(kafés métrios vrastós)

Preparation time: 10 minutes.

1   small cup of water
1   teaspoonful of sugar
1-1½ teaspoonfuls of coffee

Put the 'briki' on to heat, add the ingredients. Stir. Then allow to boil to dissipate the froth.

Greek Cheeses

The right cheese is a superb supplement to any meal, from the simplest to the most elaborate. It can be served before the main course, as a mezes, or at the end: a plate of different cheeses can be an ideal companion while the wine keeps flowing.

Greeks have been making cheese since Homeric times: the 'Odyssey' gives a complete description of how it was produced in those days.

The Greek market can offer a wide range of traditional cheeses and locally-made versions of foreign cheeses. Since the Greeks are great cheese-eaters, further variety is provided in the larger towns in the form of imported cheeses. These are popular despite the large local production.

The best-known Greek cheeses are as follows:

Feta: this is the most famous Greek cheese and the most ancient historically. It is made from sheep's milk, in round or square 'heads' which are then stored in wooden barrels or large tin cans. Feta is a white cheese; there are slightly piquant or tart variants, and it can be either soft or hard. Each 100 grams of feta contains 22 grams of fat, 23 grams of proteins and 294 calories.

Telemes: this is a variety of feta, usually made with cow's milk. The 'heads' are brick-shaped and the colour off-white. With the same nutritive features as feta, this is a most tasty cheese.

Manouri: manouri is a soft sheep's-milk cheese with all the fat. Cheese-makers often hold it in higher regard than feta. It is white and tasty and has to be consumed at once as it does not keep.

Mizithra: this is a variety of manouri made with whey, cream and a number of different types of milk. Each 100 grams of mizithra contains 150 calories.

Anthotiro: this is a kind of soft mizithra with all the fat (apart from the special low-fat varieties also available on the market). Full-fat fresh anthotiro contains approximately 300 calories for each 100 grams.

Kopanisti: this is a soft, easy to spread cheese with a high pepper content. It has so strong a taste that it is often served as a mezes with ouzo or dry white wine. It is made from full-fat sheep's milk which is well-salted during curing and later mixed with finely-ground red pepper.

Kaseri: kaseri is usually made from sheep's milk. It is a yellowish-white cheese with a sharp taste. This is a semi-hard cheese, sold in 7-kilo 'heads' and also in smaller sizes. Each 100 grams contains 370 calories.

Kefalotiri: this traditional hard cheese is made from a combination of sheep's and goat's milk. It is yellowish-white with small irregular holes. It is well-salted and has a strong aroma and a sharp taste. In some island areas it is still made in the manner of Byzantine times. Each 100 grams of kefalotiri contains 395 calories.

Kefalograviera: this is a hard cheese made from from cow's milk, sometimes mixed with a little sheep's milk. It is yellowish-white in colour, with a slightly sharp taste and many small holes. Each 100 grams contains 395 calories.

Graviera: the Greek gruyere. Graviera is rather like kefalograviera, though it differs in that very little sheep's milk is used. It has a sweet taste and a delicate aroma and is regarded as the most noble of Greek cheeses. It has holes the size of chickpeas and each 100 grams contains 400 calories.

Touloumotiri: this is a soft cheese, made from either sheep's or goat's milk or a mixture of both. It is kept in a sheepskin or goatskin bag and is rather like feta, with the same nutritive qualities. Touloumotiri has been made since antiquity, although today it is rather uncommon.

Greek Wines

We all know how much a good wine can add to the enjoyment of a meal. Even the best-cooked dish becomes tasteless when it is consumed all by itself, without the stimulating effect of alternating mouthfuls with sips of wine. And not only that: it was the great Greek philosopher who said that when a man drinks he becomes reconciled, first and foremost, with himself.

Now, of course, we do not drink only to feel better ourselves, but also because wine —quite apart from its beneficial action and its wealth of mineral salts— helps human relations and is of great importance in social life.

An aperitif such as ouzo, accompanied by a good range of mezedes, can be an excuse to invite friends in, while wine livens up the daily meal and is essential on special occasions. In the introductions to each chapter in this book, we have been giving advice as to the wines which are thought to be most suitable for certain types of food. Before going on to specific wines, there is a golden rule to remember:

when choosing wine for a light meal, select a light-bodied wine; when the dish is sharper in taste, choose a more distinctive wine. The wine ought to take its cue from the strongest taste on the table. If, for example, you are going to serve fish, but serve it with a sauce rich in pepper, then choose your wine to match the sauce, not the fish.

The vine grows everywhere and is cultivated everywhere in Greece: on flat arable land and on rocky slopes. As a result, the varieties of wine available in each area depend on the quality of the soil and there are as many tastes as there are types of grape. Most producers still use traditional methods in making their wine. As you travel across Greece, try the local wine wherever you go. You will find wine of all types and qualities, some of it bottled and some served draught, from the barrel. Representative samples of the wines of different areas can be tried each year at the NTOG Wine Festivals. Generally speaking, the wines of Crete are rough, those of the Dodecanese are sweet and those of Macedonia powerful.

Some of the Greek wines

Retsina: resinated wine, which must be drunk young, is made in Attica, Boeotia (Viotia) and Euboea (Evvia).

Rombola: a white wine from Cephallonia, bottled and sold under a large number of trade names.

Zitsa: a white, semi-sparkling wine from Epirus.

Mavrodafni: a rich red dessert wine. This sweet wine is made in number of different parts of Greece.

Also of interest are the **Samiotiko** dessert wine, the **Verdea** wines of Zakynthos, the white and red wines produced on Santorini and the varieties made in Rhodes, Nemea and Naousa. There is a wide choice of local white, rosé and red wine on the Greek market, and many brands are exported too. The range of tastes is exciting and original; if the role of wine in stimulating good humour is appreciated all over the world, it is treasured in Greece more than anywhere else. This, after all, is the country in which Dionysus, ancient god of the vine, had more 'kefi' than any other deity — and his spirit lingers on!

The Greek household of bygone days

In olden days, the Greek household worked on the basis of a calendar to plan the supply of food for the whole year. In the days when there were no freezers and refrigerators —when at last they came to Greece— were used to meet the most immediate of needs, each household had stores of foodstuffs, drinks and sweets made at a specific time of year, the time when the fruit or vegetable on which they were based was in season.

Today, the marketplace overflows with goods of all kinds and there is of course no need to make our own 'trachanas', preserves, liqueurs, or salted and pickled food. Some people still take pleasure in making such things, for their own use or to surprise their friends. If you are that sort of person, perhaps these recipes will help you to become a small-time producer in your own right. They're easy to make and a source of great pleasure!

The olive and its fruit

The pure oil of the olive is not just a rich and healthy food for modern man; it is one of the gifts of nature which the Greeks have enjoyed since very ancient times. Knowing its beneficial effects, they used it as a medicine and as a cosmetic, not only as food. After washing, the ancient Greeks would rub their bodies with olive oil to keep their skin in good condition. And at the Olympic Games the winners received crowns of olive branches, in recognition of the value this commodity had.

The harvesting of the olive begins all over Greece —wherever there are olive groves— in the month of October. There are so many different kinds and qualities of olive that the shops are full of a vast variety of table olives. The greater part of the harvest, however, goes to the olive press to be made into oil. The olive oil of Greece —much of which is exported— is of such high quality that it is the most commonly used among the fats and oils which can be employed in cooking. Its vitamins make it a nutritious food in its own right; there were times, in the past, when a slice of bread dipped in oil might be a full meal. The chapter on vegetable dishes in this book has already provided plenty of opportunities to try natural tastes in combination with olive oil. But we have something more: recipes for how to preserve your olives in the most tasty ways possible!

green olives in vinegar
(eliés prásines xidátes)

5	kilos of large, green olives
5	kilos of water
500	grms of salt
2	litres of vinegar
1 ½	litres of oil
2	litres of water
200	grms of salt

Put the olives in a large bowl of water after having nicked each one on one side. Allow to stand for 20 days, changing the water every day. Then prepare a solution with the 500 grms of salt and 5 litres of water and allow the olives to stand in this for 10 days. After the 10 days, empty this brine and prepare another solution with the 2 litres of water and the 200 grms of salt. Add to this solution the vinegar and oil and allow the olives to stand in this for 3 days. They are then ready.

salted olives
(eliés pastés)

5	kilos of good quality green or black olives
5	litres of water
250	grms of salt
150	grms of sugar

Wash the olives well and put them into a large, earthenware pot or equally large glass jar. Prepare the pickling brine. This means a solution of water and salt which is poured over the olives. The liquid should cover the olives in the container. Every other day for 2 weeks change the liquid, making the same solution of water and salt, but using 150 grms of salt and 50 grms of sugar on the last occasion. Allow the olives to stand for 2 months in this solution before consuming.

Pickles

Greek pickles are food (usually vegetables) preserved in brine — that is, in water to which salt and vinegar have been added. Preparations of this kind are natural, healthy and easily digestible. We give four representative recipes:

pickled red pepper
(piperiés kókkines toursí)

Preparation time: 30 minutes.

2	kilos of large red peppers
1	small cabbage
4-5	carrots
1	stick of celery
10	cloves of garlic

Chop finely in a large basin the cabbage, the celery, the carrots and the cloves of garlic. Salt this mixture and mix well. Wash the peppers and cut a slit on one side of each pepper, filling it with the cabbage mixture. Then place the peppers in a glass jar, cover with vinegar and add salt. After 15 days the peppers are ready and can be kept for much longer if wished.

pickled green pepper
(piperiés prásines toursí)

Preparation time: 30 minutes.

2	kilos of small, green pickling peppers
2	litres of vinegar
4-6	soupspoonfuls of salt

Wash the peppers and puncture with a fork in 2-3 places. Place them in a glass jar or earthenware container. Cover with the vinegar, which should have been mixed with the salt beforehand. Place something heavy on top.

After 20 days they will be ready. You can then put them in a glass container adding a brine solution and then covering with oil, which should be visible on the surface up to 1 centimetre.

pickled octopus
(chtapódi toursí)

1 portion calories: 200.
Preparation time: 60 minutes.

1	octopus, 1½ kilos
2	cups of water
2	cups of vinegar
10	peppercorns
	oil

Wash the octopus well and cut into pieces. Put the pieces on to heat and stir constantly with a wooden spoon. When the moisture has been absorbed, add 2 cups of water and allow to boil. When this water is also absorbed, add the vinegar and the peppercorns. Allow to boil with the vinegar until this also is absorbed. When it has cooled, put the octopus in a glass jar and cover with oil.

pickled aubergines
(melitzanáki toursí)

1 portion (3 aubergines), calories: 54.

2	kilos of small aubergines
2	sticks of celery
1	large bunch of parsley
2	heads of garlic
2	onions, 1 cup of salt
2	litres of vinegar

Wash the aubergines well, nick vertically and remove a little of the pulp. Chop the parsley, the pulp, the onions, the garlic and the celery. Put these ingredients into a large bowl and mix well. Stuff each aubergine with this mixture and tie each one with a vein from the celery stallks. Place the aubergines in an earthernware pot. Cover them with vinegar and add salt.

Drinks

mandarin liqueur
(likér mandaríni)

5	orange peels
5	mandarin peels
1	litre of ouzo
1 ½	litres of brandy
3	glasses of sugar
2	glasses of water

Put the peels into a glass jar with the 1 litre of brandy and allow to stand for 20 days. Then prepare a syrup with the sugar and water. Allow to boil together for 10 minutes. Remove the peels from the brandy and mix the brandy and syrup in a large bowl. Add the other half litre of brandy and the ouzo to the bowl. The drink is ready to be bottled.

apricot liqueur
(veríkoko likér)

240	apricot stones
2	litres of brandy
1 ½	kilos of sugar
4	glasses of water
	the juice of 1 lemon

Break the stones, put them into the brandy in a jar and seal the lid tightly; allow to stand. Put the jar in a sunny place for the whole summer. When the time comes to prepare the drink, make a syrup with the sugar and the water by boiling together and then adding the lemon juice. Allow to boil for 10-15 minutes and mix with the brandy which has been strained through muslin or filtered by another method, then serve in bottles.

morello liqueur
(likér apó víssino)

1	kilo of black cherries
1	kilo of sugar
1	litre of brandy
2	sticks of cinnamon
4	cloves

Wash the cherries well, drain and put them in a jar with the sugar. Allow this jar to sit in the sunlight for one month. Then open the jar and add the brandy, the sticks of cinnamon and the cloves. Allow the jar to remain for a further twenty days in sunlight. The liquor will be ready. Before drinking, strain through a filter or gauze, then pour into bottles.

Variation: If you wish the liqueur to have a

mavrodaphni cocktail
(cocktaíl mavrodáphnis)

2	parts mavrodaphni sweet wine
1	part morella (black cherry) liqueur
1	part brandy

Mix the ingredients well and serve with plenty of ice.

flavour other than that of cinnamon and cloves, you can omit these and use instead essence of bitter almonds. It can be found on the market in small bottles. Add 2-3 teaspoonfuls to the liqueur when it is ready to be bottled.

Spices and herbs

Anything which can give a dish added taste and aroma is important, but it should not change or spoil the dish's natural taste. Rather, it should enrich it and underline it. All the recipes in this book contain some of the herbs and spices which follow — in small but very important quantities.

The herbs and spices which grow wild or in cultivated form in Greece are very many in number. Let us look more closely at them: they have much more to give us than just a little added taste.

Parsley: the most common of all herbs. Parsley is always used fresh, which enables it to retain all its goodness. It is rich in vitamin C, and acts as a stimulant, to the appetite and to the system in general. It has medicinal uses.

Celery: the whole of this plant is used in Greek cooking, including the leaves. It is high in vitamins and other useful chemicals.

Mint: an aromatic herb with very pleasant smell. It has medicinal and deodorant qualities.

Dill: a vegetable with a very characteristic aroma. It is much used in cooking and also has considerable medicinal properties.

Basil: this ornamental and highly-scented plant is easy to grow under most conditions; apart from its unique aroma, it is also a mild stimulant.

Oregano: the powerful aroma of this plant, which grows wild, is its most striking feature. The essential oils which it contains have medicinal properties.

Rosemary: rosemary has a unique and slightly bitter taste which makes it irreplaceable in those dishes which call for it. It also has medicinal qualities and is used as a cosmetic for skin and hair.

Bay: the leaves of the bay tree are used in many Greek dishes, and add much to their taste. However, this is not their only use, for the essential oil of the bay has numerous practical and medicinal properties.

Capers: this appetising addition to salads —which also contributes to their appearance— is the pickled bud of the caper plant. It has a characteristic bitter taste and is rich in vitamin C, which means that it is beneficial to many aspects of the functioning of the body.

Onions: although onions do not strictly speaking fall into this category of foodstuff, they are so useful in Greek cooking that they really are the number one factor in flavour. Onions have many beneficial effects, notably on the heart, the nerves and the digestive system. They are also slightly soporific.

Garlic: the somewhat off-putting smell of garlic does an injustice to a plant with many important properties. It is naturally antiseptic and stimulating, which makes it useful in the treatment of a number of illnesses. Even in antiquity, when it was first cultivated, garlic was regarded as extremely important because it was food and medicine combined.

Infusions

Camomile: the flowers of this aromatic plant, which carpets the Greek countryside in spring, is antiseptic, tranquillising and a good infusion for conditions of the stomach and bowels. When making the infusion, allow one teaspoonful of herb for each cup of water.

Sage: the leaves of the sage plant, which is common in the Greek mountains, make a digestive infusion which is antiseptic and slightly stimulating. It is also used as a cosmetic for the hair. A teaspoonful of the herb is enough for one cup of infusion.

Peppermint: the flowering tops of the mint plant and its fresh leaves are used to make an infusion with a pleasant taste which is good for the digestion and has a slightly stimulating effect. Use one teaspoonful of herb to make one cup of infusion.

Bee balm: the bee balm plant (folia mellisae) grows all over Greece and scents the air. The infusion made from the flowering plant by boiling it for one minute (one teaspoonful to each cup) is useful in relieving stomach pain, aches in the joints and nervous disorders.

Eucalyptus: the leaves of this fine tree contain an essential oil which is used as an antiseptic in treating conditions of the lungs. The infusion from the leaves is a pleasant drink which is stimulating and good for the digestion. When applied externally, it combats infection and helps heal wounds.

Aniseed: the seeds of the plant, when boiled, produce an infusion which stimulates the digestive system and has a pleasant taste. Apart from essential oils, it also contains considerable amounts of calcium.

Measuring materials

The ordinary medium-sized teacup is the basic unit of measurement in the recipes in this book. The table which follows provides some conversions to help those who prefer to use other systems of measurement.

1   cup of flour equals 16 (dessert) spoonfuls or 120 grams
1   cup of milk equals 16 spoonfuls or 225 grams
1   cup of sugar equals 16 spoonfuls or 225 grams
1   cup of olive oil equals 16 spoonfuls or 225 grams
1   cup of honey equals 16 spoonfuls or 350 grams
1   cup of water equals 16 spoonfuls or 240 grams
1   cup of rice equals 225 grams
1   cup of semolina equals 175 grams
1   cup of grated cheese equals 110 grams
1   cup of cream equals 225 grams

1   dessert spoonful equals 3 teaspoonfuls
1/4 of a cupful equals 4 dessert spoonfuls

1   cup of spring onions requires 8 onions
1   cup of onions, finely chopped, requires 1 large onion
1/2 cup of onions, finely chopped, requires 1 medium-sized onion.

Oven temperatures

250 F   or 120   C   very slow
300 »   or 150   »   slow
350 »   or 177   »   medium
375 »   or 180   »   medium-hot
400 »   or 205   »   hot
450 »   or 232   »   very hot

Index

Gods & heroes
of **GR€€K**
MYTHOLOGY
embellish a
New
deck of cards
just on the market

The best gift from Greece

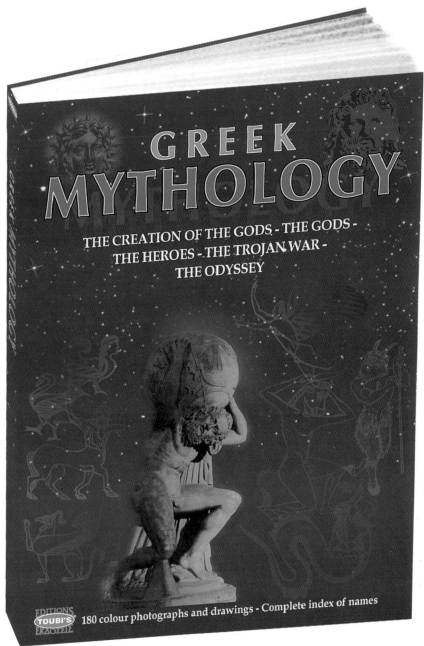

GREEK
MYTHOLOGY

This special edition has been designed to present the main Greek myths. A work of considerable scope, written in a simple and expressive language, it is accompanied by 180 photographs and excerpts from ancient Greek literature.

be sure it's from